Inhaltsverzeichnis

Vorwort

Was erwartet dich in der Prüfung? 4
Wie arbeitest du mit diesem Heft? 5

Training Section

Schriftliche Prüfung, Teil 1
Hörverstehen

1. Ablauf und Bewertung der Prüfung 6
2. Typische Aufgabenformate in Berlin und Brandenburg 6
3. Umgang mit Verständnisproblemen 10
4. Hörverstehen – *Now you* 13

Schriftliche Prüfung, Teil 2
Leseverstehen

1. Ablauf und Bewertung der Prüfung 15
2. Typische Aufgabenformate in Berlin 15
3. Leseverstehen – *Now you* 18

Schreiben und Sprachmittlung/Mediation

1. Ablauf und Bewertung der Prüfung 24
2. Typische Aufgabenformate in Berlin 25

Mündliche Prüfung
Sprechen

1. Ablauf und Bewertung der Prüfung 32
2. Typische Aufgabenformate in Berlin und Brandenburg 33
3. Sprechen – Prüfungsbeispiele 36
4. Sprechen – *Now you* 39

Musterprüfungen

Musterprüfung 1 41
Musterprüfung 2 56

Tipps für die Prüfung 71
Übersicht über die Aufgaben zum Hörverstehen 72

Lösungen (als Einleger in der Mitte des Heftes)

Training Section 2
Musterprüfungen 5

Die zentrale Prüfung Englisch im Überblick

Die Prüfung im Fach Englisch besteht in Berlin und in Brandenburg aus einem **schriftlichen Teil**, der zentral gestellt wird, und einem **mündlichen Teil**, in dem eine Englisch-Lehrerin oder ein Englisch-Lehrer das Prüfungsgespräch anleitet. Einige Prüfungsteile sind in beiden Bundesländern gleich oder ähnlich, andere unterscheiden sich (siehe Übersicht). Hilfsmittel wie z. B. Wörterbücher oder elektronische Geräte sind nicht erlaubt.

Berlin
- In Berlin kannst du, je nachdem, wie viele Punkte du in den Prüfungen erreichst, den Abschluss auf dem Niveau der Erweiterten Berufsbildungsreife (EBBR – mindestens 25 von 75 Punkten) oder auf dem Niveau des Mittleren Schulabschlusses (MSA – mindestens 45 von 75 Punkten) erlangen.
- Der schriftliche Teil dauert 150 Minuten und umfasst zu gleichen Teilen Hörverstehen, Leseverstehen und Schreiben (inklusive Mediation). Er wird mit einer Zensur bewertet und geht in der Regel zu 60 % in deine Abschlussnote ein. Um im schriftlichen Teil eine 4 zu erreichen, benötigst du 60 % der Punkte.
- Der mündliche Teil („Überprüfung der Sprechfertigkeit") ist eine Partnerprüfung und dauert je nach Anzahl der Prüflinge (2 oder 3) 10–15 Minuten. Er wird ebenfalls mit einer Zensur bewertet und geht in der Regel zu 40% in deine Abschlussnote ein.

Brandenburg
- Die Prüfung ist eine Bedingung für die Erweiterte Berufsbildungsreife (EBR), die Fachoberschulreife (FOR) oder die Berechtigung zum Besuch der gymnasialen Oberstufe. Für die verschiedenen Abschlüsse gelten unterschiedliche Bewertungsmaßstäbe.
- Der schriftliche Teil dauert 45 Minuten und umfasst nur das Hörverstehen. Die Hörverstehensprüfung ist für die EBR und die FOR identisch mit der Hörverstehensprüfung in Berlin und zählt 20%.
- Der mündliche Teil ist eine Gruppenprüfung, dauert 15–20 Minuten und zählt ebenfalls 20 %.
- Die restlichen 60 % deiner Abschlussnote errechnen sich aus deiner Jahresnote im Fach Englisch*.

		Kompetenz	Ausgangstexte und Aufgaben	Zeit
SCHRIFTLICH	**Teil 1**	Hörverstehen	vier Hörtexte mit folgenden Aufgabenformaten: · Auswahlaufgaben (*Multiple choice* mit Text oder Bildern) · Zuordnungsaufgaben (*Matching*) · Notizen anfertigen (*Note-taking*)	45 Minuten
			Pause	30 Minuten
	Teil 2	Leseverstehen	drei Lesetexte mit folgenden Aufgabenformaten: · Zuordnungsaufgabe (*Matching*) · Auswahlaufgaben (*Multiple choice*)	105 Minuten
		Schreiben (inkl. Mediation / Sprachmittlung)	drei Schreibaufgaben: · Kurztext (*Chat*) zu einem Bild verfassen · E-Mail oder Forumsbeitrag beantworten · Mediation: Informationen aus einem deutschen Text in Form einer E-Mail sinngemäß ins Englische übertragen	
MÜNDLICH		Sprechen **Berlin**	vier Aufgaben: · *Warming up (Small talk)* · *Agreeing and disagreeing* (Partnergespräch) · *Describing a picture* (monologisch) · *Discussing a topic* (Partnergespräch)	10–15 Minuten (2–3 S)
		Sprechen **Brandenburg**	drei Aufgaben: · Interview (*Small talk*) · Monologisches Sprechen (anhand eines Bildes) · Dialogisches Sprechen (Gruppendiskussion)	15–20 Minuten (2–4 S)

---

*Dies gilt, wenn du beide Prüfungsteile (schriftlich und mündlich) im Fach Englisch ablegst. Legst du die mündliche Prüfung in einer anderen Fremdsprache ab, so zählt die schriftliche Prüfung Englisch ebenfalls 20%, die Jahresnote Englisch aber 80% deiner Abschlussnote Englisch. Deine mündliche Prüfung in der anderen Fremdsprache geht dann zu 40% in die Abschlussnote dieser Fremdsprache ein.

Wie arbeitest du mit diesem Heft?

In diesem Heft lernst du durch gezielte Übungen, wie du die Aufgaben zu allen Prüfungsteilen bearbeiten kannst. Darüber hinaus bekommst du konkrete Prüfungsbeispiele. Das Heft ist deshalb wie folgt aufgebaut:

Das **erste Kapitel**, die *Training Section*, gliedert sich in die vier Kompetenzbereiche, die in der Abschlussprüfung abgeprüft werden: **Hörverstehen** und **Sprechen** in Berlin und Brandenburg sowie **Lesen** und **Schreiben** (inklusive Sprachmittlung / Mediation) in Berlin.

Die *Training Section* enthält:
* Hinweise zum Ablauf und zur Bewertung jedes einzelnen Kompetenzbereichs
* Beispiele und Tipps für alle Aufgabenformate, die in der Prüfung vorkommen können, also *Multiple choice*, *Matching* etc.
* zahlreiche Strategien zum Umgang mit typischen Schwierigkeiten, wie z. B. Verständnisproblemen
* vielfältige, prüfungsähnliche Aufgaben zum Üben *(Now you)*.

Tipp

Blau umrandete Felder markieren Tipps, die dir bei den Aufgaben helfen.

Es empfiehlt sich, die *Training Section* als erstes durchzuarbeiten, und zwar Kompetenzbereich für Kompetenzbereich. So verschaffst du dir einen Überblick darüber, was du schon gut kannst, wo du noch üben solltest und welche Strategien dir dabei helfen.

Das **zweite Kapitel** bietet dir zwei komplette **Musterprüfungen**, die jeweils alle vier Kompetenzbereiche (Hörverstehen, Lesen, Schreiben – inklusive Sprachmittlung – und Sprechen) enthalten. Sie sind den Prüfungen der letzten Jahre nachempfunden. Du lernst dadurch Schritt für Schritt die gesamte Prüfungssituation und den Aufbau einer Prüfung kennen.

Wenn du feststellst, dass du mit einem Kompetenzbereich oder einem Aufgabenformat noch Schwierigkeiten hast, gehe zurück in die *Training Section* und wiederhole gezielt die entsprechenden Übungen und Strategien oder nutze die Online-Übungen zu Grammatik und Wortschatz auf www.scook.de.

Die **Tonaufnahmen und Hörtexte** für die *Training Section* und die Musterprüfungen findest du ebenfalls online unter www.scook.de. Das Kopfhörer-Symbol mit Track-Nummer im Heft zeigt dir an, welchen Hörtext du für die Aufgabe anhören musst.

Mit dem **Lösungsteil** in der Mitte des Heftes kannst du deine Ergebnisse überprüfen und, wenn nötig, verbessern.

Nützliche Tipps zur Prüfungsvorbereitung erhältst du auf S. 71.

Nun kannst du zuversichtlich sein, dass du weißt, was in der zentralen Prüfung auf dich zukommt, und dass du die unterschiedlichen Aufgabenstellungen geübt hast und kennst.

Zusätzlich kannst du dein Grundwissen in den Bereichen Grammatik und Wortschatz mithilfe von Online-Übungen wiederholen und vertiefen. Nutze dazu den Zugangscode auf Seite 1 (www.scook.de).

Ebenfalls online findest du die Tonaufnahmen zu den Höraufgaben als MP3-Downloads, die Hörtexte sowie die Originalprüfungen früherer Jahre mit Lösungen. Nutze dazu ebenfalls den Code von Seite 1.

Viel Spaß beim Training mit diesem Heft und viel Erfolg bei der Prüfung!

Schriftliche Prüfungsarbeit, Teil 1: Hörverstehen

1. Ablauf und Bewertung der Prüfung

Der Ablauf beim Hörverstehen

Für den Prüfungsteil **Hörverstehen** hast du 45 Minuten Zeit. Er ist in Berlin und Brandenburg identisch.

Das **Hörverstehen** besteht aus vier Teilen:

Part 1: Short messages: Hier sollst du aus kurzen Nachrichten (z. B. Lautsprecherdurchsagen, Mailbox-Nachrichten) oder Dialogen detaillierte Informationen heraushören. Zu jeder Frage erhältst du vier Antworten – meist Bilder – zur Auswahl *(Multiple choice)*.

Part 2: Radio ads: Hier geht es darum, eine Reihe von vorgegebenen Slogans einzelnen Radio-Werbespots zuzuordnen *(Matching)*. Entscheidend ist, dass du die Hauptaussage des Spots verstehst.

In **Part 3** hörst du wichtige Informationen aus Monologen oder Dialogen heraus und notierst sie in einer Tabelle *(Note-taking)*.

In **Part 4** verfolgst du eine Diskussion oder Talkshow und wählst Meinungen, Gefühle oder Informationen einzelner Gesprächsteilnehmer aus vorgegebenen Antwortmöglichkeiten aus *(Multiple choice)*. Dieser Teil ist besonders anspruchsvoll und wird in der Originalprüfung mit einem Sternchen (*) gekennzeichnet.

Du hörst alle Hörtexte und die jeweilige Arbeitsanweisung zweimal. Hilfsmittel wie Wörterbücher oder elektronische Geräte sind beim Hörverstehen nicht erlaubt.

Die Bewertung der Aufgaben zum Hörverstehen

Für jede richtige Antwort erhältst du einen Punkt, und insgesamt kannst du beim Hörverstehen 25 Punkte erreichen.

Bei Aufgaben, wo du Notizen machen sollst (Part 3), brauchst du keine Angst vor Grammatik- oder Rechtschreibfehlern in deinen Antworten zu haben. Solange ein englischer Muttersprachler verstehen würde, was du geschrieben hast, gehen sprachliche Fehler in diesem Prüfungsteil nicht in die Bewertung ein.

Pass aber auf: Wenn deine Antwort länger ist als die meist vorgegebenen fünf Wörter oder Zahlen, so bekommst du den Punkt für diese Antwort nur, wenn alle von dir aufgeführten Stichworte inhaltlich richtig sind.

Bei allen anderen Hörverstehensaufgaben (Parts 1, 2 und 4) wähle immer so viele Antworten aus, wie die Aufgabenstellung fordert, selbst, wenn du nur wenig verstanden hast. So nutzt du die Chance, zufällig die richtige Antwort auszuwählen.

Das Hörverstehen macht in Berlin ein Drittel der schriftlichen Prüfungsarbeit (und 20 % der Gesamtnote) aus. In Brandenburg zählt die Hörverstehensprüfung ebenfalls 20 % der Gesamtnote.

2. Typische Aufgabenformate in Berlin und Brandenburg

In diesem Kapitel lernst du die typischen Aufgabenformate kennen, die dich bei der Abschlussprüfung im Bereich Hörverstehen erwarten.

Beachte: Die Hörtexte in der *Training Section* dienen als Beispiele für bestimmte Aufgabenformate. Sie sind daher teilweise deutlich kürzer als in der Abschlussprüfung. Längere Hörtexte findest du im Kapitel *Now you* und bei den Musterprüfungen.

Die Tipp- Kästen enthalten nützliche Strategien, wie du mit häufigen Schwierigkeiten umgehen kannst.

Listening Part 1: Short messages (Multiple choice)

Tipp

In der Prüfung hörst du in **Part 1** zwei kurze Hörtexte (Nachrichten, Dialoge).
Du musst zu jedem Hörtext je zwei Fragen beantworten, indem du das richtige Bild ankreuzt. **Ablauf:**
- Du hörst die Arbeitsanweisung.
- Du hast ca. 30 Sekunden Zeit, um die Fragen zu lesen und die Bilder anzuschauen.
- Du hörst beide Hörtexte direkt hintereinander und beantwortest dabei die Fragen.
- Du hast ca. 10 Sekunden Zeit, um deine Antworten zu überprüfen.
- Du hörst beide Hörtexte ein zweites Mal. Dabei kannst du deine Antworten nochmals prüfen.

a) Bearbeite zunächst die Aufgabe im Tipp-Kasten.

Tipp

Gleich hörst du einen Beispieldialog. Nutze die kurze Zeit vor dem ersten Hören und bereite dich anhand der Bilder darauf vor, was du im Hörtext hören könntest. Hier:

1 Wie lauten die dargestellten Uhrzeiten?
   A: _____   **B:** _____   **C:** _____   **D:** _____

2 Welche Wörter erwartest du?   **A:** *pool, swimming*   **B:** ?   **C:** ?   **D:** ?

 b) Nun höre den Beispieldialog zu **Listening Part 1** an und bearbeite die Aufgabe wie in der Prüfung gemäß Arbeitsanweisung im blauen Kasten.

- *You are going to hear a short dialogue.*
- *You will hear the recording twice.*
- *There are two questions.*
- *Look at the pictures and then listen to the recording.*
- *Choose the correct picture and put a tick (✓) in the right box.*

Tipp

Ausschlussverfahren: Wenn du nicht gleich auf die richtige Antwort kommst, weil du manche Wörter im Text nicht verstanden hast, überlege, welche Lösungen auf jeden Fall falsch sind.

1 At what time are they planning to meet?

A ☐   **B** ☐   **C** ☐   **D** ☐

2 What are they planning to do?

A ☐   **B** ☐   **C** ☐   **D** ☐

Listening Part 2: Radio ads (Matching)

Tipp

In der Prüfung hörst du in **Part 2** vier Radio-Spots. Du musst jeden Spot einem von sechs Slogans zuordnen. Zwei Slogans bleiben übrig. **Ablauf:**
- Du hörst die Arbeitsanweisung.
- Du hast 30–40 Sekunden Zeit, um die Slogans zu lesen.
- Du hörst alle vier Spots direkt hintereinander und kreuzt in der Tabelle den passenden Slogan an.
- Du hast ca. 10 Sekunden Zeit, um deine Antworten zu überprüfen.
- Du hörst alle vier Spots ein zweites Mal.

a) Lies zunächst die Empfehlungen und die Aufgabe im Tipp-Kasten.

Tipp

Gleich hörst du vier Radio-Spots als Beispiel. Vorher liest du die sechs Slogans (**A–F**) unten. Dabei ist wichtig:

Du wirst diese Slogans in den Radio-Spots nicht wörtlich hören. Es geht vielmehr darum, dass du Sinn und Absicht der Werbung erfasst. Im ersten Spot wirst du z.B. Wörter aus dem Bereich „Essen" hören: *chicken*, *tomatoes*, *mushrooms* etc. Das könnte auf Slogan **A** hindeuten. **Aber:**

Es ist gefährlich, nur aus Einzelwörtern auf eine Lösung zu schließen! Überlege stattdessen: Worum geht es in diesem Spot eigentlich? Was ist die Gesamtsituation? Passt das immer noch zu Slogan **A**?

 b) Nun höre die Beispiel-Spots zu Listening **Part 2** und bearbeite die Aufgabe wie in der Prüfung gemäß Arbeitsanweisung im blauen Kasten.

Please note: You do not need to understand every word to do this task.
- *You are going to hear four radio ads.*
- *You will hear the recording twice.*
- *Read the slogans below first, then listen to the recording.*
- *For each ad choose the correct slogan from the list (A–F) and put a tick (✓) in the right box.*
- *There is only one correct slogan for each ad.*
- *Two slogans can't be matched.*

A   Eat healthily.

B   Work in an old people's home.

C   Buy ethical cosmetics.

D   Stay active.

E   Advice for bird owners.

F   Recycle.

Radio ads	Slogan					
	A	B	C	D	E	F
Radio ad 1	☐	☐	☐	☐	☐	☐
Radio ad 2	☐	☐	☐	☐	☐	☐
Radio ad 3	☐	☐	☐	☐	☐	☐
Radio ad 4	☐	☐	☐	☐	☐	☐

Listening Part 3: Calgary's skyways (Note-taking)

Skyway in Calgary

3

- You are going to hear a radio report about the skyway network in Calgary, a city in western Canada.
- You will hear the recording twice.
- Complete the table below. Use 1 to 5 words or numbers.

	Length (km)	Height above ground (m)	Called the +15 because ...	Advantage *(name one)*	Disadvantage *(name one)*
Calgary's skyways	1	2	3	4	5

* Listening Part 4: A visit to Krakow (Multiple choice)

4

- You are going to hear a conversation between Tim and a friend.
- You will hear the recording twice.
- Read the statements below first, then listen to the recording.
- Put a tick (✓) in the box next to the correct statement.
- Only one statement is correct in each case.

1 Tim travelled to Krakow	**A** ☐	by train.
	B ☐	by plane.
	C ☐	by car.

2 In Krakow Tim stayed	**A** ☐	with a family member in a village.
	B ☐	with a friend in the town centre.
	C ☐	in town, but not in the centre.

3 In Krakow Tim visited	A	☐	places with few tourists.
	B	☐	the main tourist sites.
	C	☐	places with not too many people.

Tipp

Vorsicht bei identischen Wörtern in Hörtext und Aufgabe! Sie deuten nicht unbedingt auf die richtige Lösung hin.

Beispiel: Im Hörtext kommt *main tourist sites* vor – wie in Lösung **B**. Ist **B** folglich die richtige Lösung? Nein! Wie könnte das zu erklären sein?

4 In Krakow Tim made himself understood with English and	A	☐	no Polish, but lots of smiles.
	B	☐	a little Polish and making signs.
	C	☐	Polish that he had learnt at school.

Tipp

Bei Multiple-Choice-Aufgaben werden einzelne Wörter aus dem Hörtext oft ersetzt durch:
- **Synonyme** (Wörter und Ausdrücke mit ähnlicher Bedeutung, wie *great – wonderful*)
- **Antonyme** (Wörter und Ausdrücke mit gegensätzlicher Bedeutung, wie *great – awful / not great at all*)

Dieses Wissen kann dir helfen, die richtige Lösung zu finden, z. B. in Aufgabe **5**. Welcher Ausdruck im Hörtext …
- ist ein Synonym zu *everybody should visit Krakow* in **A**? *It's a _____ destination.*
- ist ein Antonym zu *should know a few words of Polish* in **B**? *You _____ the language.*

5 Tim thinks that	A	☐	everybody should visit Krakow.
	B	☐	every visitor should know a few words of Polish.
	C	☐	both **A** and **B**

6 Tim thinks that	A	☐	Krakow is changing fast.
	B	☐	Krakow is becoming more expensive.
	C	☐	both **A** and **B**

3. Umgang mit Verständnisproblemen

Die Hörtexte in der Abschlussprüfung enthalten manchmal Wörter, die du vielleicht nicht kennst oder die du nicht verstehst, weil sie von anderen Geräuschen im Prüfungsraum überdeckt werden. Das ist ganz normal. Also keine Panik – es gibt Strategien, die dir helfen, die wesentlichen Inhalte trotzdem zu erfassen und die Aufgabe zu lösen. In diesem Kapitel werden anhand eines Werbefilms über die Niagarafälle die wichtigsten Strategien vorgestellt. Diese Strategien kannst du auch für die Aufgaben zum Leseverstehen nutzen.

The Niagara Falls

- *You are going to hear the audio track of a publicity film about the Niagara Falls.*
- *Read the statements below first, then listen to the recording. You can read the text while you listen.*
- *Put a tick (✓) in the box next to the correct statement (tasks 1–5).*
- *Only one statement is correct in each case.*
- *At the end you will hear the text again (task 6).*

Tipp

Die Tonaufnahme (🎧 5) enthält Störgeräusche, die einige Textstellen unverständlich machen. Im Hörtext sind diese Stellen durch Schwärzungen kenntlich gemacht.

Dieses Vorgehen soll dir verdeutlichen, dass du einige der Aufgaben 1–5 trotz der fehlenden Textstellen lösen kannst. Bei anderen Aufgaben kannst du mithilfe der Tipps zumindest Vermutungen anstellen.

Beim zweiten Hören (🎧 6) in Aufgabe 6 hörst du den Text ohne Störgeräusche. Nun kannst du überprüfen, ob deine Vermutungen richtig waren.

Welcome to the Niagara Falls! These astonishing natural waterfalls are on the border between the USA and Canada. They consist of three waterfalls. The two smaller ones are in the USA. But these amazing falls, called the Horseshoe Falls, are the biggest and they're ▮▮▮▮ in Canada. The Niagara Falls are located near important urban centres. It only takes half an hour by car to get to Buffalo.

These tourists have just landed at Buffalo International Airport and they're on their way to see the famous falls. In fact, about 30 million people visit the Niagara Falls each year! This group is going on the very popular *Maid of the Mist* tour – a boat tour to the bottom of the waterfalls. The air here is full of ▮▮▮▮▮ ▮▮▮▮▮▮▮▮▮ – that's why everyone here is wearing ▮▮▮▮▮▮▮▮. But don't be fooled – most of them are going to get wet anyway. Oh! Here comes the next shower!

Accessing the falls is easy. That's great because it means that thousands of people can come and see the fantastic sight. But it also means that the falls have to be well protected and taken care of. In fact, these falls on the American side are actually part of ▮▮▮▮▮ ▮▮▮▮▮ state park. It was designed by the same man who laid out this well-known park.

Do you recognize it? It's Central Park in New York City. Luckily state parks don't charge entrance – so you don't have to pay to see the falls. Tourists can stand right next to the top of the Horseshoe Falls and watch the water spilling over. Isn't it amazing?

Sometimes people have gone over the falls. Some have even done it by choice. This is Annie Taylor – she was the first person to ride over the Niagara Falls, way back in 1901, on her 63rd birthday. After her husband and son had died, Annie was facing poverty and decided to go over the falls ▮▮▮▮▮▮▮▮▮. And guess what she used to cross the falls: this thing. That's right – a wooden barrel. The sort of barrel that was used to store wine or beer. Crazy, isn't it? She put cushions and a mattress inside and asked some friends to push the barrel in the right direction at the top – and other friends to open it when she got to the bottom of the falls. And she did: she went over the top of the falls, the barrel fell, and when her friends opened it, she was alive. But although Annie (amazingly!) came out with no broken bones, she ▮▮▮▮ ▮▮▮▮▮: it was bleeding. After her crazy experiment, Annie warned other people against doing the same thing. We'll take your advice, Annie.

Line numbers: 5, 10, 15, 20, 25, 30, 35, 40, 45, 50, 55

1 The Horseshoe Falls	A	☐	are smaller than the American falls.
	B	☐	are fully in Canada.
	C	☐	are for the most part in Canada.

Tipp

Wenn du nicht gleich auf die richtige Antwort kommst, wende das Ausschlussverfahren an:
- Markiere die Stelle im ersten Absatz, die Antwort **A** ausschließt.
- Zwischen **B** und **C** kannst du dich noch nicht entscheiden: Im Hörtext könnte es nämlich heißen *only in Canada*, **mainly** *in Canada*, **partly** *in Canada* oder **fully** *in Canada*.

Also wirst du nochmals hören müssen. Aber jetzt kannst du gezielt zwischen zwei möglichen Antworten entscheiden – das ist leichter als zwischen dreien.

2 To protect themselves, the people on the boat are wearing	A	☐	helmets against head injuries.
	B	☐	raincoats against the water.
	C	☐	safety gloves.

Tipp

Hier kannst du dir helfen, indem du Vermutungen anstellst:
Wovor müssen sich die Touristen wohl schützen? Gefahren für Kopf und Hände sind im Hörtext nicht erwähnt. Dafür erfährst du aber, dass die Touristen _____ werden. Wie kann man sich davor schützen?

Achte beim 2. Hören besonders gut auf diese Stelle. Mit dieser Vorbereitung wirst du sie bestimmt besser verstehen.

3 The land on the American side of the falls	A	☐	can only be reached if you pay.
	B	☐	was the first state park in the USA.
	C	☐	looks like Central Park in New York City.

Tipp

Wende das Ausschlussverfahren an!
Lösung **C** kannst du sogar, wenn du fast nichts verstanden hast, mit dem gesunden Menschenverstand ausschließen. Warum?

Lösung **A** kannst du ebenfalls ausschließen, wenn du die relevante Stelle im Text verstanden hast. Markiere diese Stelle.

4 Annie Taylor went over the falls in a barrel in order to	A	☐	raise money.
	B	☐	show that women could be brave.
	C	☐	become famous.

Tipp

Was weißt du über Annie Taylor? Kannst du daraus schließen, zu welchem Zweck sie so etwas Gefährliches gemacht hat?

5 When Annie Taylor's friends opened the barrel, they found that she was	A	☐	dead.
	B	☐	injured.
	C	☐	unhurt.

Tipp

• Markiere das Wort im Hörtext, mit dem du Lösung **A** ausschließen kannst.
• Das Wort *although* im Text leitet einen Gegensatz ein: Obwohl sie nichts gebrochen hatte, war sie _____.
Dank dieses Wortes kannst du also beim 2. Hören zwischen Lösung **B** und Lösung **C** wählen. Siehst du wie?

6 Listen to the programme again. This time it's complete. Note the exact words in the recording.

a) ... the Horseshoe Falls are the biggest and they're _____ in Canada.

b) ... everyone here is wearing _____ .

c) ... these falls on the American side are actually part of _____ state park.

d) Annie (...) decided to go over the falls to _____ .

e) But although Annie (amazingly!) came out with no broken bones, she _____

_____ – it was bleeding.

7 Now use your information from task **6** to check your answers to tasks **1–5**.

Niagara Falls on USA side

4. Hörverstehen – *Now you*

In diesem Kapitel kannst du die Strategien, die du auf den letzten Seiten kennen gelernt hast, bei ausgewählten Aufgaben zum Hörverstehen gezielt üben. Grundlage dafür sind ein Dialog über ein Radrennen in Yorkshire und eine Reportage über Sehenswürdigkeiten in Brighton.

The Tour de Yorkshire

- *You are going to hear a conversation between Sarah from Ireland and Mo from Yorkshire.*
- *They are talking about a cycling race called the* Tour de Yorkshire.
- *You will hear the recording twice.*
- *Read the statements below first, then listen to the recording.*
- *Put a tick (✓) in the box next to the correct statement.*
- *Only one statement is correct in each case.*

Yellow bicycle on the city walls of York, 2014

1 In 2014 the *Tour de France* cycling race	A	☐	began in France and came to Yorkshire.
	B	☐	went through other countries and then came to Yorkshire.
	C	☐	began in Yorkshire.

2 During the stages of the race in Yorkshire	A	☐	cycling fans rode yellow bicycles on the sides of the roads used by the race.
	B	☐	people bought lots of yellow bicycles.
	C	☐	there were old yellow bicycles on the sides of the roads used by the race.

3 The organizers of the *Tour de France*	A	☐	planned for large crowds.
	B	☐	didn't expect the enthusiastic reaction from people in Yorkshire.
	C	☐	hoped that many people would join the cyclists.

4 The *Tour de France*	A	☐	was in Yorkshire for 21 days.
	B	☐	left people in Yorkshire wanting to see more cycling races.
	C	☐	went from Yorkshire directly on to France.

5 The *Tour de Yorkshire* cycling race	A	☐	includes hills that are difficult even for experienced cyclists.
	B	☐	uses wide roads to allow for big groups of cyclists to pass through.
	C	☐	has become a very popular off-road race.

Three tourist attractions in Brighton

- *You are going to hear descriptions of three tourist attractions in Brighton.*
- *You will hear the recording twice.*
- *Complete the table below. Use 1 to 5 words or numbers.*

British Airways i360

The Royal Pavilion

	When built / opened?	Why built?	What can you see?	Price
British Airways i360	*August 2016*	*to keep the tourists coming*	**1** _____ _____	**2** £ *15* for tourists or £ ____ for _____ _____
Royal Pavilion	**3** between _____ and _____	**4** _____ _____ _____	**5** _____ _____ _____	**6** £ ____ for _____ or £ ____ for _____
Brighton sewers	*1860*	**7** _____ _____ _____	**8** _____ _____ _____	**9** £ ____ for _____ or £ ____ for _____

Schriftliche Prüfungsarbeit, Teil 2: Leseverstehen

1. Ablauf und Bewertung der Prüfung

Der Ablauf beim Leseverstehen

Das **Leseverstehen** gehört – zusammen mit dem Schreiben – zum **zweiten Prüfungsteil**, für den du insgesamt 105 Minuten Zeit hast. Dieser zweite Teil wird nur in Berlin geprüft. Wörterbücher oder andere Hilfsmittel sind in der Prüfung nicht erlaubt.

Beim **Leseverstehen** gibt es drei Teile mit Texten, zu denen du Aufgaben bearbeitest:

Part 1: eine Zuordnungsaufgabe *(Matching)* zu mehreren kürzeren Texten: Du ordnest verschiedenen Personen passende Angebote zu, z.B. Aktivitäten, Urlaubsorte, Filme oder Jobs.

Part 2: Du bearbeitest Auswahlaufgaben *(Multiple choice)* zu mehreren kürzeren Texten (z.B. Reklame, Warnschilder, Hinweistafeln).

Part 3: Du bearbeitest Auswahlaufgaben *(Multiple choice)* zu einem längeren, anspruchsvolleren Text (mit*).

Die Bewertung der Aufgaben zum Leseverstehen

Zu den Lesetexten in Parts 1, 2 und 3 gibt es insgesamt 25 Aufgaben *(Multiple choice* oder *Matching)*, für deren richtige Beantwortung du jeweils einen Punkt bekommst, sodass du insgesamt 25 Punkte erreichen kannst.

Das Leseverstehen macht in Berlin ein Drittel der schriftlichen Prüfungsarbeit (und 20 % der Gesamtnote) aus.

2. Typische Aufgabenformate in Berlin

In diesem Kapitel lernst du die typischen Textsorten und Aufgabentypen kennen, die dich bei der Abschlussprüfung im Bereich Leseverstehen erwarten.

Beachte: Die Lesetexte in der *Training Section* dienen als Beispiele für bestimmte Aufgabenformate. Sie sind daher teilweise kürzer als in der Abschlussprüfung. Längere Lesetexte findest du in den Musterprüfungen.

Die Tipp-Kästen enthalten nützliche Strategien, wie du mit typischen Schwierigkeiten umgehen kannst.

Reading Part 1 (Matching)

Die erste Leseverstehensaufgabe in der Prüfung ist eine Zuordnungsaufgabe: Du liest fünf Personenbeschreibungen. Anschließend ordnest du diesen Personen sieben Texte zu (jeder Person zwei Texte, wobei meist einige Texte mehrfach zugeordnet werden können). Um dieses Aufgabenformat kennenzulernen und zu üben, geht es hier in der *Training Section* zunächst nur um drei Menschen und sechs Aktivitäten (A–F), wobei jede Person nur einer Aktivität zugeordnet werden muss.

Holiday activities

- *These young people (a–c) want to take part in a holiday activity.*
- *First read the information about the people, then look at the descriptions of the activities (A–F) on page 16–17.*
- *In each case find the activity each person would want to do. Write the letter of the activity in the box next to the person's name.*
- *Each activity can only be chosen once.*

No.	Activity	The people	
1			**a)** **Karen** loves discovering and exploring new places. Her financial resources are limited, so she is prepared to put up with fairly basic accommodation. She is more interested in spending time with like-minded people, as eager as she is to tackle new experiences and challenges.
2			**b)** **Jack** is a sports freak, and does well in everything from football to climbing, from kayaking to camping. He does well in both team and individual sports. But while he loves doing sport himself, his passion during the holidays is to share these skills with children from deprived areas of the country.
3			**c)** **Celina** is into arts and crafts of all kinds. She makes her own clothes, she restores and paints old furniture, and she has even done a course in colouring glass. Rather than doing more of a skill in which she is already well versed, however, she prefers to test herself against new challenges.

A

The Buxton Sports Academy offers holiday courses in a range of sports that include sailing, tennis, climbing, boxing and squash, as well as team sports such as football, rugby and hockey. Professional coaches who are used to working with young people give a thorough training and develop each individual's skills.

> **Tipp**
>
> Jack mag Sport – und doch ist **A** nicht die richtige Antwort. Er sucht etwas anderes. Siehst du, was?
>
> _____

B

Many families have old chairs or faded chests of drawers up in the attic or out in the garden shed – pieces of furniture that were once a source of pride and joy, and which could become so again. This 5-day residential course teaches students how to remove old paint and varnish, how to deal with stains and woodworms, and how to bring colour back into faded wood. Suitable for beginners or experienced wood workers.

> **Tipp**
>
> _Furniture_ kommt bei Celina vor – und doch ist **B** nicht das passende Angebot für sie. Warum nicht?
>
> _____

C

Fancy a special adventure? Then join us on the expedition of a lifetime: a rail journey from London to Singapore!
We'll take the train to Moscow, then the Trans-Siberian Railway to Beijing (six nights on the train). After spending one night in Beijing, we'll continue via Hanoi and Ho Chi Minh City (formerly Saigon) in Vietnam, from where there are frequent bus connections via Phnom Penh to Bangkok in Thailand.
The final journey is a two-night trip to Singapore by train. Cost of the trip: £4999.

> **Tipp**
>
> Wow! Was für eine tolle Reise, und Karen mag Reisen. Und doch ist **C** nicht die richtige Antwort für sie. Warum nicht?
>
> _____

D

The Haxby Pottery Farm runs residential pottery courses for all ages and abilities. Create your own pots or sculptures, and make vases for your home or ceramic presents to give away. It's a great way to develop your pottery skills or learn a new craft, and make new friends. Phone Edna on 01826 34591 for more details.

Tipp

Pots, vases, sculptures ... kommen bei keinem der drei Teenager vor. Die Gesamtsituation ist aber wichtiger als Einzelwörter. Warum passt sie am besten zu Celina?

_____

E

Every year we run a two-week residential camp in August in the heart of the Derbyshire Dales for in-ner-city children from the Greater Manchester area. The children have been selected by social workers working with families in some of the poorest inner-city wards, with the aim of giving the children new opportunities and their parents a break.

We always need volunteer assistants to help us run the courses: we cover board and lodging, but can offer no pay.

Tipp

Zu wem passt dieser Text – und warum?

_____

F

Three intrepid hikers are looking for a fourth member to join them on a ten-day hike in the Italian Alps. Overnight stays in mountain huts and shelters, or in tents if necessary.

We have an old car to get us to Italy and kindly ask for a contribution to the cost of the fuel.

Tipp

Zu wem passt dieser Text – und warum?

_____

Reading Parts 2 and *3 (Multiple choice)

In der Prüfung bearbeitest du auch Auswahlaufgaben zu mehreren kürzeren Texten (Part 2) und dann zu einem längeren, anspruchsvolleren Text (Part 3). Die Hilfen, die du hier bekommst, gelten für beide Arten von Text.

Australia's Stolen Generations

Read the texts on page 18. They are from a museum about the history of Aboriginal people in Australia.

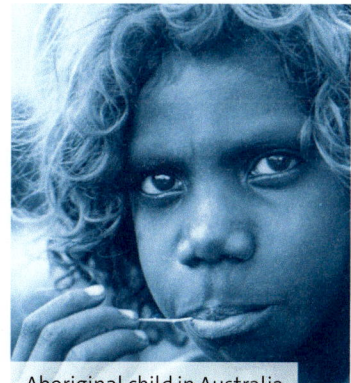

Aboriginal child in Australia

- *Look at the text and the statements in each task.*
- *Put a tick (✓) next to the statement that matches the text – A, B, C or D.*
- *There is only one correct statement for each text.*

Tipp

Bei Multiple-Choice-Aufgaben werden einzelne Wörter aus dem Lesetext oft ersetzt durch:
- **Synonyme** (Wörter mit ähnlicher Bedeutung, wie *pretty – beautiful*)
- **Antonyme** (Wörter mit gegensätzlicher Bedeutung, wie *pretty – ugly*)

Dieses Wissen kann dir helfen, die richtige Lösung zu finden, z.B. bei Aufgabe **1** (Seite 18):

Zu *forced to stay* in **1C** gibt es im Text ein Antonym, nämlich _____ . **C** ist daher wahrscheinlich falsch.

In the mid-20th century the Australian government adopted a new policy known as the indigenous child removal policy and officials began to take Aboriginal children away from their mothers and fathers, usually by force.

This was the fate of over 250,000 Aboriginal children, some say as many as 500,000, who had to leave their homes.

1 What happened to thousands of Aboriginal children?

A	☐	They died of disease.
B	☐	They were removed from their parents.
C	☐	They were forced to stay with their parents.
D	☐	They wanted to leave their parents.

Tipp

Ein **Aktivsatz** im Text kann zu einem **Passivsatz** bei den Aufgaben werden (oder umgekehrt):

bei den Aufgaben:	im Text:
Passiv **1B** They _were removed_ from …	**Aktiv** … children _had_ to _____ their homes.
Aktiv **2A** They _had to eat_ food …	**Passiv** They were _____ the foods …

The children from Aboriginal families were housed in new English-speaking homes where they were not allowed to speak their own language. And they were given the typical foods of white Australians, even though they weren't used to it.

2 What was life in their new homes like?

A	☐	They had to eat food that was new to them.
B	☐	Aboriginal and white Australians learned each other's languages.
C	☐	Aboriginal children had to speak their own language.
D	☐	Everybody got the food they liked best.

Tipp

- **Vorsicht bei identischen Wörtern** in Lesetext und Aufgabe! Im Lesetext kommt _speak their own language_ vor – wie in Satz **2C**. **2C** ist aber nicht die richtige Lösung. Warum nicht?

_____

3. Leseverstehen – _Now you_

In diesem Kapitel kannst du die Strategien, die du auf den letzten Seiten kennen gelernt hast, bei ausgewählten Aufgaben zum Leseverstehen gezielt üben.

Reading Part 1: Work practice (Matching)

- _These young people (a–e) have to do work practice in a business or company._
- _First read the information about the people, then look at the work practice offers (A–G) on page 19–20._
- _In each case find the **two** work practice offers that would suit each person best. Write the letters of the offers in the boxes next to the people's names._
- _Some of the work practice offers can be chosen more than once._

No.	Offer 1	Offer 2	The people	
1/2				**a)** **Jonny** is fascinated by all things that grow. He loves analysing leaves and flowers with his microscope, but he's even happier when he can follow up his interest out of doors and he loves driving to sites of scientific interest. Unfortunately, his old car often breaks down, so Jonny is keen to improve his skills as a mechanic.
3/4				**b)** **Samina** started making things when she was only three years old. She had phases of knitting, and now she loves working creatively with wood, making both stand-alone works of art and practical objects for around the house. But her creative skills stretch into the virtual world too, and Samina has recently begun creating websites.
5/6				**c)** As though it isn't enough that **Tadek** speaks fluent Polish, German and English, he is also teaching himself Arabic and Japanese. He loves talking with people, and languages, he says, are the key to meeting people. He's particularly impressed that young children can communicate so easily and would like to have the opportunity to study this phenomenon for himself.
7/8				**d)** **Katja** loves making cakes, brownies and biscuits, and experiments by making different sorts of bread. Not surprising that her favourite TV show is *The Great British Bake Off*! And from cake decorating she has branched out into garden design. She loves TV shows which show how gardens are transformed with new plants and decoration, and she would like to know more about everything that has got to do with gardening.
9/10				**e)** **Zoe** is a friendly and tolerant person who loves getting to know people from different countries. But one thing makes her really angry and that is poor website design. She can't stand sites that look boring, are difficult to use or have information that is out of date. "There's no excuse for it," she says. "It's easy enough to produce an attractive web design – even quite a complicated one."

A City Tours

Tourists come to our city from all over the world, and many want to know more about our city's fascinating history. Here at *City Tours* we provide walking tours in an ever-growing number of different languages. Do your work experience here and you are sure to engage with interested clients from around the globe.

B Horace's Garden Centre

We are the largest garden centre in town, with the widest choice of trees, shrubs and plants. We are happy to train students who share our passion for everything that grows in the garden. In addition to working at the till, you will learn how to breed plants from seeds and how to pack plants safely for orders by post.

C K&J Logistics (formerly Lipton Removals)

We have been in the business of moving homes for over 100 years and enjoy an enviable reputation for reliability. We deal both with moves in and around our city and moves to countries abroad, and we have recently developed a new branch for renting out vans. Your work experience will of course involve carrying some furniture, but we'll also give you useful advice on looking after van and lorry engines.

D Techs United

This is a young and innovative company, and if you decide to do your work experience here you'll find yourself working with people not much older than yourself! Some will be working on new computer games, others will be developing apps for customers as varied as *Bright Day Biscuits* and *Featherstone Tyres*. What unites us is a passion for good quality digital work – and if you have good ideas in this field, we'll be happy to hear them!

E Little People Nursery

We provide a safe, happy environment for preschool children from a range of different ethnic and linguistic backgrounds. We open at 7 am each workday and can look after your baby or toddler for an hour or two, or all the way through till we close at 6 pm. All our assistants are qualified and of course we provide all children with snacks and meals.

F Kevin the Carpenter

I taught technology for several years before setting up a new business as a carpenter. My first orders were for chairs and window frames, but I now carry out special orders like garden cabins and church pews. My two assistants and I will show you how to use a wide range of tools and help you to practise a range of skills. Come and join the team!

G Pattercakes Bakery

We opened our shop three years ago, when Lauren spotted the lack of a baker's shop in this part of town. Since then we have grown to be rather successful, with our fresh bakery products flying off the shelves. Come and join us for your work experience, and you'll pick up baking tips and tricks that will be useful to you for life.

Reading Part 2: Short texts (Multiple choice)

- *Look at the text and the statements in each task.*
- *Put a tick (✓) next to the statement that matches the text – A, B, C or D.*
- *There is only one correct statement for each advert.*

Melissa Pahlavi worked for three years in South America and took amazing photos at archaeological sites such as Machu Picchu. Her stunning photographs are now on show in the City Library. The exhibition runs until the end of November.

Open 10 am to 5 pm

Pay what you like.

1

A	☐	A museum is showing South American paintings.
B	☐	You can buy a special book about South America at the library.
C	☐	A photographer is giving a talk about Machu Picchu.
D	☐	You can choose how much money you want to give to see a collection of photos.

Tickets to watch the England v Pakistan cricket match next May are currently on sale.

This sure-to-be-exciting game will be an important part of England's preparation as they seek to win the *Test Series* later in the year.

Tickets: Adult £45-£65, U16 £15-£25

Order your tickets online. Don't miss out: we predict that this event will be sold out by the end of November.

2

A	☐	Tickets for the match will be on sale starting in May.
B	☐	There are tickets available for the match, but probably not for long.
C	☐	If you buy your ticket online, you will be sure to get one.
D	☐	Tickets for this match were gone at the end of November.

Lead up to a sparkling Christmas as you skate on real ice at the annual outdoor skating rink in the yard opposite the Castle.
And every Wednesday and Sunday evenings our rink becomes the coolest dance floor in town during special disco sessions.

All our prices include skate hire. Book online and get over 10% off.

Since 1999!

3

A	☐	This event takes place in an old castle, on real ice.
B	☐	You can try your dancing skills on ice twice a week.
C	☐	Christmas ice skating is in town for the first time.
D	☐	Tickets only cost 10% more if you need to hire the skates.

Rich Pickings at the Polo Theatre

One actor. One hour. One of the funniest shows you'll ever see. Barbara Newman is incredible in this solo role, in which she investigates the life of investors, bankers and accountants in the City of London. Hilarious, passionate, hard-hitting – this is a show you'll never forget.

7.30 pm from Monday to Saturday, 2 pm matinee on Saturday, 26 November. £12.

4

A	☐	*Rich Pickings* is performed only in the evening.
B	☐	The actors are so good that you'll always remember this show.
C	☐	Rich Pickings is a very talented comedian.
D	☐	A woman is making fun of business people in London.

*Reading Part 3: Filming in New Zealand (Multiple choice)

- *Read the text and the statements on page 23.*
- *Put a tick (✓) in the box next to the correct answer.*
- *Only one answer is correct in each case.*

New Zealand's breathtaking landscape has long attracted the world's top film directors.

The *Lord of the Rings* trilogy, for example, was filmed in different areas of New Zealand, mainly, though not exclusively, in the country's national parks. The films made use of spectacular mountains such as Mount Ngauruhoe, a treeless live volcano, and of rivers, lakes and wild canyons. But scenes were also filmed in the softer and less dramatic looking green hills near Matamata.

One of the advantages of filming in New Zealand is that the population density is so low, with only four and a half million people in a country more or less the same size as the United Kingdom (population: 64 million). So there are fewer buildings, roads and power lines to spoil the views of open countryside.

Disney's award-winning family movie *Pete's Dragon*, produced in 2015, also made good use of New Zealand's cinematographic landscape. The producer required giant redwood trees, a wild river where a bear could scare the hero, and bare mountains with cliffs from which a dragon could appear. All this was filmed in New Zealand, too. The wonderfully-named Whakarewarewa Forest near Rotorua has Californian redwood trees, the McLaren Falls Park features the wild river and the dramatic Deer Park Heights near Queenstown provided the remote and rugged mountains needed. And a helicopter company based in Queenstown helped to film the scene where the dragon flew over the mountains – not the only example of how filming brings employment to more than just actors and producers.

The Lord of the Rings – The Fellowship of the Ring (USA/NZ 2001)

Indeed, many of the visual effects that make the dragon so lifelike were created in digital animation offices in Wellington, New Zealand's capital and second largest city – which has itself featured in a number of films. In the 2005 remake of the film classic *King Kong*, for example, many of the scenes supposedly set in New York were actually filmed in Wellington.

This means that the southernmost capital city in the world has a thriving film industry and professional experience of working with some leading film directors in the world.

Mount Ngauruhoe, New Zealand

1	A		in various regions of New Zealand.
The *Lord of the Rings* trilogy was filmed	B		in national parks only.
	C		in just one part of New Zealand.
	D		on Mount Ngauruhoe only.

2	A		in wild hills near Matamata.
All the scenes of the *Lord of the Rings* were filmed	B		in spectacular and less spectacular scenery.
	C		on a volcano famous for its trees.
	D		in the most dramatic parts of the country.

3	A		fewer people per square kilometre than the United Kingdom.
New Zealand has	B		about as many people per square kilometre as the United Kingdom.
	C		more people per square kilometre than the United Kingdom.
	D		about the same number of inhabitants as the United Kingdom.

4	A		was partly filmed in the city of Wellington.
Disney's movie *Pete's Dragon*	B		gave work to a local company that flies helicopters.
	C		brought redwood trees from California to New Zealand.
	D		both B + C

5	A		is New Zealand's biggest city.
Wellington	B		is further south than any other capital city.
	C		has good scenery, but no local film industry.
	D		all of them (A + B + C)

Schriftliche Prüfungsarbeit, Teil 2: Schreiben

1. Ablauf und Bewertung der Prüfung

Der Ablauf beim Schreiben

Das **Schreiben** gehört – zusammen mit dem Leseverstehen – zum **zweiten Prüfungsteil**, für den du insgesamt 105 Minuten Zeit hast. Dieser zweite Teil wird nur in Berlin geprüft. Wörterbücher oder andere Hilfsmittel sind in der Prüfung nicht erlaubt.

Zum **Schreiben** gehören drei Teile:

Part 1: Du schreibst einen kurzen Text (30–50 Wörter) über ein gepostetes Foto.

Part 2: Du reagierst auf einen Blog-Eintrag oder einen Beitrag in einem Internet-Forum und nimmst in einer längeren E-Mail (mindestens 100 Wörter) begründet zu einem Thema Stellung.

Part 3: Du wählst aus einem deutschen Text für eine andere Person interessante Informationen aus und gibst diese in einer englischsprachigen E-Mail sinngemäß wieder (Mediation).

Die Bewertung beim Schreiben

Das Schreiben macht in Berlin ein Drittel der schriftlichen Abschlussprüfung aus (und 20 % der Gesamtnote).

Für Part 1 bekommst du maximal 5 Punkte, für Part 2 gibt es 12 Punkte und für Part 3 kannst du 8 Punkte erreichen.

Die Punkte beim Schreiben werden je zur Hälfte für **Inhalt** und **Sprache** vergeben. Der Bereich **Sprache** beinhaltet:
- Grammatik: Satzbau, Verbformen, Präpositionen usw.
- Wortschatz: Kenntnis vieler Vokabeln, ihre richtige Anwendung, die Verwendung von Redewendungen
- Rechtschreibung (auch Groß- und Kleinschreibung)

Um im Bereich **Sprache** die **volle** Punktzahl zu erreichen, ist eine klare sprachliche Darstellung entscheidend. Du darfst nur wenige Fehler machen, musst einen umfangreichen Wortschatz richtig verwenden und einen anspruchsvollen Satzbau unter Beweis stellen.

Für den Bereich **Inhalt** musst du **alle** in der Aufgabenstellung verlangten Aspekte bearbeiten. Wenn du eine E-Mail verfasst, achte auch auf eine passende Anrede und Schlussformel und einen guten einleitenden und abschließenden Satz.

Auch für den Bereich **Inhalt** ist es sehr wichtig, verständlich zu schreiben, und zwar für eine Person, die nur Englisch, aber kein Deutsch spricht.

2. Typische Aufgabenformate in Berlin

In diesem Kapitel lernst du die typischen Aufgabenformate kennen, die dich bei der Abschlussprüfung im Bereich Schreiben erwarten. Die Tipp-Kästen enthalten nützliche Hinweise und Hilfen.

Writing Part 1: Your photo

a) **Arbeitsanweisung:** Lies dir die Arbeitsanweisung genau durch und bearbeite die Aufgabe im Tipp-Kasten.

- *You have posted this photo.*
- *Your friend Sarah wants to know more.*
- *Answer her questions.*
- *Write 30 – 50 words.*

Great photo! Where did you take it?
Who is she?
And what's she doing?

Tipp

Für deine Aufgabe gibt es maximal 5 Punkte. Um 3, 4, oder 5 Punkte zu bekommen, **musst du alle drei Fragen** beantworten.

Markiere also die Schlüsselwörter in den drei Fragen. So verlierst du keine Punkte, weil du versehentlich eine Frage übersehen hast.

Was sind hier die Schlüsselwörter?

_____

b) **Sprache:** Du bekommst Punkte für deine **klare sprachliche Darstellung.** Es geht also darum, so wenige Fehler wie möglich zu machen.

Wie könnte deine Lösung aussehen? Hier ist ein Beispiel.
Aber Achtung: Die blau markierten Wörter sind fehlerhaft.
Lies die Hinweise in den Kästen und verbessere die Fehler.

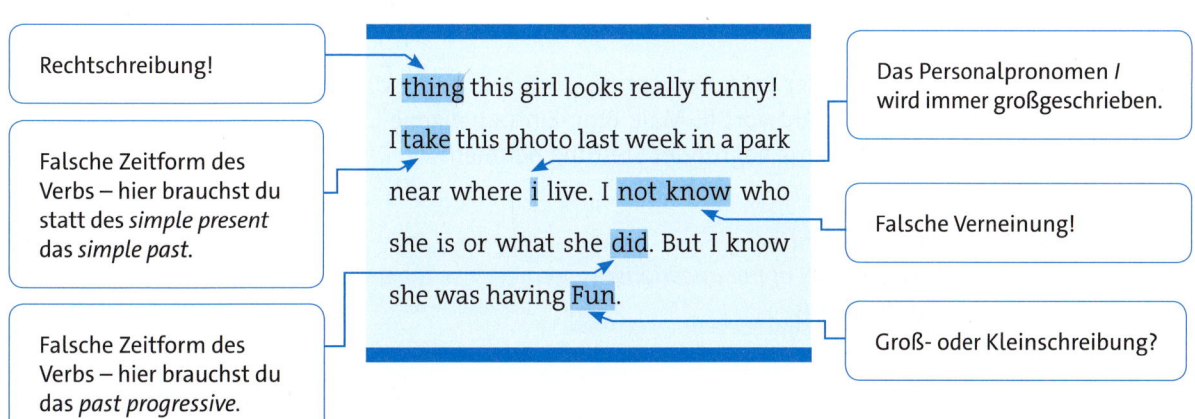

Rechtschreibung!

Falsche Zeitform des Verbs – hier brauchst du statt des *simple present* das *simple past*.

Falsche Zeitform des Verbs – hier brauchst du das *past progressive*.

I thing this girl looks really funny!
I take this photo last week in a park near where i live. I not know who she is or what she did. But I know she was having Fun.

Das Personalpronomen *I* wird immer großgeschrieben.

Falsche Verneinung!

Groß- oder Kleinschreibung?

Tipp

Schau dir noch einmal deine letzten drei Klassenarbeiten an. Erstelle eine Checkliste mit acht bis zehn Fehlern, die mehrmals aufgetaucht sind. Beispiel:

wrong: *right:*

I ~~not like~~ this.   →   *I don't like this.*

Sieh dir diese Liste immer wieder an, um diese Fehler in Zukunft zu vermeiden.

c)   **Dein Text:** Nun schreibe deinen eigenen Text.
Schau dir dafür noch einmal die Arbeitsanweisungen in **a)** an.

d)   **Überprüfe** deinen Text auf mögliche Fehler.
Nimm dir am Ende der Prüfung Zeit, deine Texte noch einmal zu überprüfen. Wir machen alle Fehler beim Schreiben. Jede Korrektur, die du hier machen kannst, bringt dir Punkte.

Inhalt	Sprache
Hast du die drei Fragen beantwortet: – Wo wurde das Foto gemacht? – Wer ist die Person? – Um was für eine Situation handelt es sich? Hast du 30 bis 50 Wörter geschrieben?	Stimmen die Zeitformen der Verben? Sind alle Wörter richtig geschrieben? Hast du auf Groß- und Kleinschreibung geachtet? Hast du irgendwo ein falsches Wort verwendet? Stimmen der Satzbau und die Verneinungen?

e)   **Jetzt bist du Prüferin oder Prüfer!**
Du kannst fünf Punkte vergeben wenn...
- die Antworten **zu allen drei Fragen** sprachlich klar formuliert sind
- kaum Fehler im Text sind
- der Bezug zur Aufgabe immer erkennbar ist
- der Text zwischen 30 und 50 Wörter lang ist.

Tipp

Es ist immer leichter, Fehler bei anderen zu finden! Daher ist es eine sehr gute Übung, Texte von einem Partner oder einer Partnerin zu überprüfen.

Nun lies deinen Text oder den deines Partners noch einmal und entscheide, wie viele Punkte der Text verdient.

Punkte: _____

Begründung: _____

Writing Part 2

Bei der zweiten Schreibaufgabe der Prüfung liest du zunächst einen kurzen Blog- oder Forumseintrag. Anschließend sollst du in deiner Antwort (E-Mail, Blog-Eintrag) eigene Erfahrungen beschreiben und zu einem (oftmals kontroversen) Thema begründet Stellung nehmen.

- *Read what the blogger has written.*
- *Then write back, answering all of her questions.*
- *Write a minimum of 100 words.*

Eigene Erfahrungen beschreiben

a) Lies den Blog-Text, zu dem du dich äußern sollst. Damit du nichts übersiehst, ist es immer hilfreich, die Stellen im Text zu markieren, die dir sagen, worüber du schreiben sollst. Am besten nummerierst du die Fragen und machst dir zu jeder Frage ein paar Notizen.

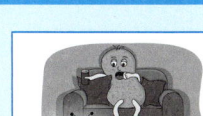

Name: **CouchPotato**

At weekends I'm perfectly happy to stay at home, reading, playing games, watching films, or just chilling. But some of my friends think I'm just lazy. They think a great weekend must be an active weekend. So maybe you can help me.
Can you tell me your idea of what makes a great weekend? Any ideas?
Can you describe your greatest weekend ever? And tell me why it made you feel so good? And can you tell me what you think of somebody who prefers to be at home?

1 Can you tell me your idea of what makes a great weekend? (Any ideas?)

a weekend spent outside

2 Can you describe your greatest weekend ever?

camping trip with Sam

3 And tell me why it made you feel so good?

highest mountain I ever climbed – proud

4 And can you tell me what you think of somebody who prefers to be at home?

b) Die ersten drei Fragen (**1–3**) fordern dich hier dazu auf, deine eigenen Erfahrungen zu schildern. Lies den Beispieltext rechts und bearbeite folgende Aufgaben:

Satzbau: Nebensätze bringen Punkte, weil sie über einfache Satzmuster hinausgehen. Markiere die Nebensätze mit einem Textmarker.

Grammatische Strukturen: Die abwechslungsreiche und korrekte Verwendung verschiedener grammatischer Strukturen bringt Punkte. Unterstreiche:
- die Verneinung von zwei Verben
- zwei Verben im *past perfect*

Unterkringele:
- ein Adjektiv in der Superlativform
- vier oder mehr Verbindungswörter *(linking words)*

Wortschatz: Notiere hier:
- Verben (im *simple past*, also der Zeitform, in der du vergangene Erlebnisse schildern musst):

- Adjektive:

A great weekend for me is a weekend spent outside. Last weekend, for example, I went with my friend Sam on a camping trip in the mountains. Actually, my friend Dave had wanted to come too, but he didn't have time because he had so much homework.

We hiked along muddy valleys, we climbed steep hills and in the evening we cooked on an open fire. Although the weather was awful, it was great fun. The wet nights weren't great, but it was a wonderful feeling when I stood on the highest mountain that I had ever climbed!

c) Beantworte nun die ersten drei Fragen aus dem Blog für dich selbst und beschreibe dabei deine eigenen Erfahrungen. Schreibe ca. 70 – 90 Wörter.

Begründet Stellung beziehen

d) Bei der letzten Frage aus dem Blog (**4**) geht es eher um deine persönliche Meinung: Was hältst du von Menschen, die – wie die Bloggerin – das Wochenende lieber zuhause verbringen? Diese Meinung sollte sich logisch aus deinen zuvor geschilderten Erfahrungen ergeben.

Im Beispieltext könnte die Antwort auf die letzte Frage der Bloggerin so aussehen:

Schau dir auch diesen Text im Hinblick auf die folgenden Bereiche an, deren gute Umsetzung Punkte bringen.

Inhalt: Markiere in unterschiedlichen Farben:
- die Pro-Argumente
- die Kontra-Argumente
- das Ergebnis

Sprache: Unterstreiche verschiedene Formulierungen, um Argumente einzuführen und abzuwägen.

e) Beantworte nun die letzte Frage aus dem Blog für dich persönlich. Deine Meinung sollte zu dem passen, was du zu den ersten drei Fragen geschrieben hast. Schreibe ca. 70 – 90 Wörter.

f) Überprüfe nun deinen gesamten Text anhand dieser Checklisten:

> As an outdoor person, I think that a weekend at home is a little bit boring. For me, getting fresh air and exercise is more relaxing than chilling on the sofa. On the other hand, if the weather is bad a weekend at home can be really nice. Moreover, sometimes my week has been so full that I just don't have the time to organize a weekend activity outside. So all in all I would say that how you spend your weekend depends on many things – the season, the weather, the time available – and there's no good or bad as long as your weekend gives you energy for the new week.

Prüfe den Inhalt deines Textes:	
Ich habe alle Fragen aus dem Blog beantwortet.	☐
Ich habe insgesamt mindestens 100 Wörter geschrieben.	☐
Ich habe meine Erfahrungen beschrieben.	☐
Ich habe begründet Stellung bezogen (Argumente).	☐
Ich bin zu einem begründeten Ergebnis gekommen.	☐

Prüfe die Sprache deines Textes:	
Ich habe komplexe Sätze mit Haupt- und Nebensatz gebildet.	☐
Ich habe einen umfangreichen Wortschatz (Adjektive, Verben, …) verwendet.	☐
Ich habe verschiedene grammatische Strukturen verwendet.	☐
Ich habe abwechslungsreiche Satzanfänge geschrieben.	☐
Ich habe *linking words (and, but, so, because, on the one hand, …)* verwendet.	☐
Ich habe sowohl einen einleitenden als auch einen abschließenden Satz geschrieben.	☐
Ich habe *time words (at first, next, two hours later, during the summer, …)* verwendet.	☐
Ich habe meine Rechtschreibung überprüft.	☐
Ich habe die Grammatik überprüft.	☐

g) **Jetzt bist du Prüferin oder Prüfer!** Lies deinen Text (oder noch besser: den Text eines Partners) und entscheide, wie viele Punkte der Text verdient. Du kannst insgesamt zwölf Punkte vergeben – sechs für den Inhalt und sechs für die Sprache.

Punkte: _____

Begründung: _____

_____

Writing Part 3: Mediation

Bei der dritten Schreibaufgabe geht es um Sprachmittlung. Deine Aufgabe ist es, wichtige Informationen aus deutschen Texten ins Englische zu übertragen – du erhältst dabei in der Prüfung zwei Texte, zwischen denen du wählen kannst (hier als Beispiel nur einen). Es handelt sich dabei nicht um eine Wort-für-Wort-Übersetzung, sondern darum, die wesentlichen Informationen zu erkennen und sinngemäß ins Englische zu übertragen.

> * *Mira, a new girl in your class, does not speak German very well. She wants to improve her German by meeting young people in her free time and has asked you for help.*
> * *Read the advert for a youth centre on page 30.*
> * *Write Mira an email and tell her what the advert is about. Mention at least **four important** activities that are on offer.*
> * ***Do not translate word for word**, just give the main information.*
> * *Write complete sentences.*

a) Lies zuerst die Arbeitsanweisung gründlich und beantworte dir folgende Fragen:

* Für wen sollst du Informationen zusammenfassen?

  ein Mädchen, das ... neu in meine Klasse gekommen ist welches ihr Datsch verbessern möchte

* Welche Informationen sind gewünscht?

  vier Aktivitäten, bei denen ... sie junge Leute kennenlernen kann

* Was für einen Text (Textsorte) sollst du schreiben?

  eine E-Mail

b) Nun lies die Anzeige des Jugendzentrums auf Seite 30 und markiere die Informationen, die für Mira von Interesse sind.

> **Tipp**
>
> Fast alle Texte benötigen eine klare Gliederung mit:
> * Einleitung
> * Mittelteil/Hauptteil
> * Schluss/Ergebnis
>
> Hier sollst du eine E-Mail schreiben. Denke also zusätzlich an:
> * Anrede: *Hi/Dear/Hello ...*
> * Grußformel: *Yours/Love/Regards/Best wishes/...*
>
> Wiederhole auch die Regeln und Redemittel für persönliche oder formelle Briefe. Du findest sie bestimmt in deinem Englischbuch.

Jugendzentrum Hegeda

Im Jugendzentrum Hegeda können sich Jugendliche von 12 bis 18 Jahren treffen.
Wollt ihr einfach nur eure Freunde treffen, spielen, klönen oder einfach mal entspannen, könnt ihr das bei uns tun.

Euch stehen vielfältige Freizeitangebote wie zum Beispiel Tischtennis, Billard oder Tischfußball zur Verfügung sowie Kurse in Deutsch für Anfänger.
Mittwochs ist von 16 Uhr bis 18 Uhr Kindercafe.

Älteren Jugendlichen bieten wir Unterstützung bei der Berufsfindung, d.h. beim Bewerbungsschreiben oder bei der Lehrstellensuche.
Und wenn ihr Stress, Kummer oder Ärger mit euren Eltern, Geschwistern oder Freunden habt, sind wir für euch da.

Ihr könnt unter Anleitung Fahrräder reparieren, die Küche nutzen und euch am Kindercafe als Organisatoren beteiligen.

Alle Jugendlichen von 12 bis 18 sind auch zu unseren *Abenden der internationalen Küche* herzlich eingeladen, an denen junge Menschen aus aller Welt die Küche ihres Landes vorstellen (3,50 Euro Kostenbeitrag). Diese Abende finden ungefähr alle zwei Wochen statt.

c) Lies die Tipps und ergänze die Sätze auf Englisch.

1

> Wollt ihr einfach nur eure Freunde treffen, spielen, klönen oder einfach mal entspannen, könnt ihr das bei uns tun.

At the youth club you can meet people, you can chat and you can *relax* _____ .

> **Tipp**
>
> Schreibe die Infos in deinen eigenen Worten. Du kannst zum Beispiel diesen Satz einfach mit *you can* beginnen.
> - Die Wörter „treffen, spielen, klönen" müssen nicht in derselben Reihenfolge vorkommen.
> - Kennst du „entspannen" nicht auf Englisch? Keine Sorge – lass es einfach weg.

2

> Euch stehen vielfältige Freizeitangebote wie zum Beispiel Tischtennis, Billard oder Tischfußball zur Verfügung.

The centre also offers billiard tables, *table tennis and table football* _____ .

> **Tipp**
>
> Dieser Satz könnte auch anders beginnen, z.B.:
> *You'll find ... too.*
> Notiere weitere Vorschläge.

3

> Älteren Jugendlichen bieten wir Unterstützung bei der Berufsfindung, d.h. beim Bewerbungsschreiben oder bei der Lehrstellensuche.

The centre can help you if you're looking for a job or if you need to *write an application* _____ .

> **Tipp**
>
> Beachte immer, aus welcher Sichtweise und an wen du schreibst. Passe die Personalpronomen entsprechend an.
> → Im deutschen Text steht „wir".
> → Du schreibst *the centre* oder *they*.
> Verwende Verben, um lange deutsche Wörter wie „Berufsfindung" und „Bewerbungsschreiben" zu umschreiben:
> *If you're looking for a job or if you need to ...*

4 Und wenn ihr Stress, Kummer oder Ärger mit euren Eltern, Geschwistern oder Freunden habt, sind wir für euch da.

You can talk with somebody at the centre if _you_

have worries or problems with .
family or friends.

d) Schreibe nun die komplette E-Mail an Mira gemäß Aufgabenstellung.

e) Überprüfe nun deinen Text anhand dieser Checklisten:

Prüfe den Inhalt deines Textes:	
Meine E-Mail hat eine Anrede und eine Grußformel.	☑
Ich habe das Thema meines Schreibens genannt. (Einleitung)	☑
Ich habe vier für Mira wichtige Informationen wiedergegeben. (Mittelteil)	☑
Ich habe meine E-Mail durch ein Fazit oder eine Verabschiedung abgerundet. (Schluss)	☑

Prüfe die Sprache deines Textes:	
Meine Sprache passt zur Textsorte (E-Mail) und zur Adressatin (gleichaltriges Mädchen).	☑
Ich habe nicht Wort für Wort übersetzt, sondern eigenständig formuliert.	☑
Ich habe darauf geachtet, Personalpronomen je nach Sichtweise zu verändern.	☑
Ich habe eine Bandbreite an Wortschatz und Strukturen weitgehend fehlerfrei verwendet.	☑

f) **Jetzt bist du Prüferin oder Prüfer!** Lies deinen Text (oder noch besser: den Text eines Partners) und entscheide, wie viele Punkte der Text verdient. Du kannst insgesamt acht Punkte vergeben – vier für den Inhalt und vier für die Sprache.

Punkte: _____

Begründung: _____

Mündliche Prüfung: Sprechen

Im Folgenden geht es um die **Überprüfung der mündlichen Sprechfertigkeit** in Berlin bzw. die **mündliche Prüfung** in Brandenburg. Die Prüfungen sind sehr ähnlich, aber nicht identisch. Sie sollten nicht mit einer zusätzlichen mündlichen Prüfung verwechselt werden, die im Nachhinein abgelegt werden kann.

1. Ablauf und Bewertung der Prüfung

Der Ablauf der mündlichen Prüfung

Die mündliche Prüfung ist in **Berlin** eine **Partnerprüfung** mit zwei (in Ausnahmefällen auch drei) Schülern. Sie dauert in der Regel bis zu 12 Minuten (bei drei Prüflingen 15 Minuten) und besteht aus **vier** Teilen (Parts). In **Brandenburg** ist es eine **Gruppenprüfung** mit bis zu vier Schülern. Sie dauert zwischen 15 und 20 Minuten und besteht aus **drei** Teilen, die im Wesentlichen den Parts 1, 3 und 4 der Berliner Prüfung entsprechen. Es gibt keine Vorbereitungszeit.

Part 1: Warming up `Berlin` – Interview `Brandenburg`
Zum Einstieg beantwortest du einfache Fragen, die sich z.B. auf deine Familie, Heimatstadt, Freizeitaktivitäten, Freunde, Schule oder Zukunftspläne beziehen. Oft sollst du etwas buchstabieren (z.B. deinen Namen), manchmal kannst du selbst Fragen stellen.

Part 2: Agreeing and disagreeing `Berlin`
Du diskutierst mit einem Partner oder einer Partnerin über ein lebensnahes Thema, z.B. Arten und Weisen, ein Zimmer einzurichten oder sich fit zu halten. Hier geht es darum, Vorschläge zu machen und auf Vorschläge des Partners angemessen zu reagieren. Als Unterstützung erhaltet ihr kleine Bilder, die ihr im Gespräch berücksichtigen solltet.

Part 3: Describing a picture `Berlin` – Monologisches Sprechen `Brandenburg`
Du und dein Partner erhaltet je ein Bild (Foto, Zeichnung, Cartoon; in Brandenburg auch Diagramm, Zitat) zu einem gemeinsamen Thema und sprecht nacheinander und zusammenhängend darüber.

Part 4: Discussing a topic `Berlin` – Dialogisches Sprechen `Brandenburg`
Ausgehend vom Thema in Part 3 tauschst du mit den anderen Prüflingen deine Gedanken aus. Ihr diskutiert, wägt Argumente ab und versucht, zu einer Problemlösung zu kommen. Thematisch könnte es z.B. um die Einführung von Schuluniformen oder um ein Verbot von Fast Food an Schulen gehen.

Die Bewertung bei der mündlichen Prüfung

Die Überprüfung der Sprechfertigkeit macht in Berlin circa 40% der Gesamtnote der Abschlussprüfung aus, in Brandenburg 20%.

Deine Leistung wird anhand von vier gleichrangigen Kriterien bewertet:

Umgang mit den Gesprächspartnern	Inhaltliche Qualität des Gesprächsbeitrags	Grammatik und Wortschatz	Aussprache, Betonung, Flüssigkeit
Du ergreifst die Initiative. Du hältst das Gespräch aufrecht. Du stellst deinem Partner Fragen und gehst auf Redebeiträge des Partners ein. Du beendest das Gespräch. Du sprichst verständlich.	Deine Beiträge sind sinnvoll, begründet und angemessen. Deine Gedanken sind klar strukturiert. Du sprichst zum Thema. Du sprichst zusammenhängend.	Du verwendest grammatische Strukturen weitgehend sicher. Einzelne Fehler beeinträchtigen die Kommunikation nicht. Du verfügst über einen breiten Wortschatz, der es dir ermöglicht, über verschiedene Themen differenziert zu sprechen.	Deine Aussprache und Betonung sind so gut, dass man dich problemlos versteht. Du sprichst flüssig und mit einer natürlichen Satzmelodie.

Solltest du etwas nicht verstehen, zögere nicht, **auf Englisch** nachzufragen. Es ist wichtig, dass du alle Fragen richtig verstehst und dass keine zu langen Gesprächspausen entstehen.

2. Typische Aufgabenformate in Berlin und Brandenburg

In diesem Kapitel lernst du die typischen Aufgabenformate kennen, die dich bei der mündlichen Prüfung in Berlin und Brandenburg erwarten. Die Tipp-Kästen enthalten nützliche Strategien.

Einige Aufgaben kannst du alleine bearbeiten. Nimm dafür am besten deine Stimme auf und höre dir das Gesagte anschließend an. Da es sich um eine Partner- bzw. Gruppenprüfung handelt, ist es aber sinnvoller, dich zusammen mit einem Freund oder einer Freundin vorzubereiten.

Speaking Part 1: Warming up `Berlin` `Brandenburg`

Die Prüferin könnte fragen:

> *Hello. How are you today?*

> *What's your name?*
> *How do you spell your first/last name?*

> *Where do you live?*
> *How long have you been living there?*

> *What's your favourite food / school subject?*

> *Do you have any brothers or sisters?*

Tipp

Part 1 besteht aus Fragen, die kurz beantwortet werden können. Aber auch kurze Antworten sollten natürlich klingen, z. B. auf die Frage:

How are you today?
nicht: *Good.*
sondern: *I'm good, thanks. But I feel a bit nervous.*

Antworte nicht einsilbig, z. B. auf die Frage:

Do you have any brothers or sisters?
nicht: *No. / Yes.*
sondern: *No, unfortunately I don't. /*
           Yes, I do. My sister is ten and ...

Wiederhole das Buchstabieren auf Englisch (A/R, E/I, G/J ...). Im Internet findest du viele ABC-Songs.

Bereite dich auf Part 1 vor, indem du Mindmaps zu typischen *Small-talk*-Themen anfertigst: Pläne für die Zukunft, Hobbys etc.

Speaking Part 2: Agreeing and disagreeing `Berlin`

Der Prüfer könnte sagen:

> *I'm going to describe a situation to you:*
> *you share a flat with a friend*
> *and you decide to buy a pet together.*
> *Talk about what pet you would like*
> *and which you don't want.*
> *Here is a picture*
> *with some ideas to help you.*

Tipp

Du bekommst Punkte dafür, dass du das Gespräch aufrechterhältst:

Wäge deine Argumente ab und begründe sie, z. B.: *Dogs are good pets because ...*

Greife auf Beispiele zurück, z. B.:
Rats can be really good pets. That's surprising, isn't it? But I have a friend who has a rat, and ...

Reagiere auf das, was dein Gegenüber sagt, z. B.: *A snake? Really? Are you serious? Tell me more!*

Wiederhole wichtige Redemittel:
What do you think of ... / What about ...?
I (don't) think that's a good idea because ...
That's true, but ...
Do you agree?
All right, I agree. / I'm afraid I don't agree because ...

Speaking Part 3: Describing a picture `Berlin` `Brandenburg`

In der Prüfung bekommt jeder von euch ein anderes Bild (Foto, Grafik, Cartoon, Diagramm, ...) zur Beschreibung vorgelegt. Du sprichst ca. eineinhalb Minuten lang über dein Bild und hörst dann zu, während deine Partnerin oder dein Partner über ihr oder sein Bild spricht.

Der Prüfer könnte sagen:

> *I'm going to give each of you a picture. This is your picture, candidate A. Please show it to your partner and describe it.*

Die Prüferin könnte sagen:

> *Now candidate B, here's your picture. Please show it to your partner and tell us what you see.*

Tipp

Bei der Bildbeschreibung zählen ein breiter Wortschatz und die Verwendung einer Vielfalt an Strukturen.

Verwende unterschiedliche Satzanfänge, z. B.:

This picture shows ...
In the picture I can see some ...

(Achtung! *On* the picture ... ist falsch!)

In the right-hand corner there is/are ...

I'm not quite sure, but in the background I think I can see ...

Beschreibe, was die Menschen auf dem Bild gerade tun. Benutze dafür das *present progressive*, z. B.:

I can see people who are waiting for a bus.

Du kannst spekulieren, was die Personen im Bild gerade tun, getan haben oder tun werden, z. B.:

I think the girl with the phone is talking to her boyfriend.

The woman on the right has probably just picked up her daughter from play school.

Tipp

Du kannst auch über die Gefühle oder Gedanken der dargestellten Personen spekulieren, z. B.:

I think the man with the cap is worried about something that the man on the right is saying.

Wenn du zu früh aufhörst zu reden, wird dir der Prüfer oder die Prüferin Zusatzfragen stellen. Das ist oft viel schwieriger, denn dann bestimmt jemand anders, worüber gesprochen wird – egal, ob du den notwendigen Wortschatz nun kennst oder nicht.

Das kannst du vermeiden, indem du selber weitersprichst!

Tipp

Wiederhole die Ortsangaben:

On the left / On the right / In the middle ...

At the top / At the bottom ...

In the foreground / In the background ...

Next to / Behind / Opposite / In front of ...

Speaking Part 4: Discussing a topic `Berlin` `Brandenburg`

Der Prüfer könnte sagen:

You both have pictures which show where people live.
Now please talk together about your ideal place to live. Do you prefer a city, a small town or the country?

Tipp

Höre deinem Partner zu und schaue ihn an.

Frage nach, wenn du etwas nicht verstanden hast:
Could you say that again, please?
Sorry, what did you say?

Lasse deine Partnerin zu Wort kommen und reagiere auf das, was sie sagt:
Yes, I agree that village life can be ..., but I think ...
That's a good point. But I wouldn't like to live in town because ...

Stelle ihr Fragen:
What do you think about ...?
Well, I prefer ... What about you?

Bringe deine eigenen Erfahrungen in die Diskussion:
I live in ..., where there is ..., so I think ...
I've never lived in ..., so I don't really know what it's like. But I imagine that ...

Prüfe, ob ihr zu einem gemeinsamen Ergebnis kommen könnt:
OK, so what have we agreed on so far? Do we prefer ...?
On the one hand ..., on the other hand ...
I know I first argued for ..., but I've changed my mind. Let's agree on ... instead. OK?

Tipp

Wiederhole wichtige Redemittel zum Diskutieren:

Stating your opinion:
- *In my opinion ... / In my view ...*
- *Well, I'd say ...*
- *(Personally,) I think/feel/believe ...*
- *If you ask me, ...*
- *First of all, ...*
- *To start with, I'd like to point out that ...*

Agreeing:
- *I quite agree. / You're quite right.* (👍)
- *You've got a good point there. / I think so too.* (👍)
- *That's true. / That's just it.* (👍👍)
- *I agree completely.* (👍👍👍)
- *I couldn't agree with you more.* (👍👍👍)

Disagreeing:
- *I'm afraid I don't (quite) agree (there).* (👎)
- *I'm not so sure, really.* (👎)
- *Well, that's one way of looking at it, but ...* (👎)
- *I don't believe that at all.* (👎👎)
- *(Sorry,) I think you're wrong.* (👎👎👎)
- *I definitely disagree.* (👎👎👎)

Asking for clarification:
- *Sorry, I didn't get that.*
- *Are you saying that ...?*
- *Does your last statement mean that ...?*
- *Could you please give an example of ...?*
- *Could you say that again, please?*

3. Sprechen – Prüfungsbeispiele

In diesem Kapitel hörst du gute und weniger gute Beispiele von mündlichen Prüfungen. Werte sie aus und verbessere so deine eigene Leistung in der mündlichen Prüfung.

Speaking Part 1: Warming up

Prüfungsbeispiel 1

 Das erste Prüfungsbeispiel ist **kein gutes Beispiel**. Höre zu und bearbeite die Aufgaben.

a) Warum sind die Antworten des Kandidaten nicht gelungen? Notiere mindestens drei negative Aspekte.

b) Bei einer Antwort ist die Verbform falsch. Notiere die falsche Verbform, streiche sie durch und korrigiere sie.

Prüfungsbeispiel 2

 Das zweite Prüfungsbeispiel ist **ein gutes Beispiel**. Höre zu und bearbeite die Aufgaben.

a) Warum sind die Antworten des Kandidaten nun gelungen? Notiere mindestens drei positive Aspekte.

b) Wie verschafft sich der Kandidat Zeit zum Nachdenken, bevor er antworten muss? Notiere zwei Möglichkeiten.

Speaking Part 2: Agreeing and disagreeing

You and your friend are planning to do an activity on Saturday. Talk about what activities you would like to do and what activities you don't want to do. Here are some pictures with some ideas to help you.

Prüfungsbeispiel 1

 Das erste Prüfungsbeispiel ist **kein gutes Beispiel**. Lies zunächst die Aufgabenstellung in der Sprechblase. Dann höre zu und bearbeite die Aufgaben.

a) Welcher Prüfling ist hier kein guter Gesprächspartner? Kreuze an: Junge ☐   Mädchen ☐

b) Was macht der Prüfling nicht so gut? Notiere drei negative Aspekte.

▶ Fortsetzung (Seite 37) nach den Lösungen

ABSCHLUSS-PRÜFUNGS-TRAINER

Mittlerer Schulabschluss
Berlin und Brandenburg

Lösungen

Cornelsen

TRAINING SECTION: Hörverstehen ▶ S. 6–14

Listening Part 1: Short messages (Multiple choice)

a) Tipp:

1 A: *a quarter past eleven (a.m.) / eleven fifteen (a.m.)*

1 B: *twenty-five to two (p.m.) / thirty-five past one (p.m.) / one thirty-five (p.m.)*

1 C: *a quarter to four (p.m.) / three forty-five (p.m.)*

1 D: *a quarter past four (p.m.) / four fifteen (p.m.)*

2 B: *museum, dinosaur, history, exhibition, ...*

2 C: *store, shopping, clothes, fashion, ...*

2 D: *ice-skating, ice-rink*

b) 1: D · 2: C

Listening Part 2: Radio ads (Matching)

a) **Tipp:** Gesamtsituation: Es geht um Recycling.

b) ad 1: F · ad 2: C · ad 3: A · ad 4: E

Listening Part 3: Calgary's skyways (Note-taking)

1 *18 kilometres*

2 *4.5 metres*

3 *15 feet high / 15 feet up in the air*

4 *less rain and cold / protected from rain and cold / protected from the weather · safer for pedestrians / don't have to cross roads*

5 *less life at street level / streets feel deserted / less life in the streets / leave streets empty / ...*

*Listening Part 4: A visit to Krakow

1 B (**Tipp:** *fly, flight, airport, ...*)

2 C (**Tipp:** A + B)

3 A (**Tipp:** Aussage im Hörtext verneint: *NOT the tourist sites*)

4 B

5 A (**Tipp:** A: *It's a must-see destination.* ·
B: *You don't need to learn the language.*)

6 C

The Niagara Falls

1 C (**Tipp:** Lösung A ausschließen: *But these amazing falls, called the Horseshoe Falls, are the biggest, and ...* (Z. 5–6))

2 B (**Tipp:** Die Touristen werden *wet* (=nass). Davor kann man sich durch *Regenjacken, Regenschirme* etc. schützen.)

3 B (**Tipp:** Lösung C ausschließen: Es ist sehr unwahrscheinlich, dass die Natur um die Niagarafälle herum so aussieht wie ein Park in einer Großstadt. · Lösung A ausschließen: *Luckily state parks don't charge entrance – so you don't have to pay to see the falls.* (Z. 30-31))

4 A (**Tipp:** Wir wissen, dass Annie Taylor nach dem Tod ihres Mannes und ihres Sohnes von Armut bedroht war.)

5 B (**Tipp:** Lösung A ausschließen: *alive.* (Z. 51) · Lösung C ausschließen: Obwohl sie nichts gebrochen hatte, war sie *verletzt* (=injured). *Although* leitet einen Gegensatz ein – *unhurt* (=unverletzt) kann hier nicht der Gegensatz sein, weil der Satz dann keinen Sinn machen würde. Das Wort *although* schließt also Lösung C aus.)

6 a) *mainly* · b) *waterproof ponchos* · c) *the country's oldest* ·
d) *raise money* · e) *did hurt her head*

The Tour de Yorkshire

1 C · 2 C · 3 B · 4 B · 5 A

Three tourist attractions in Brighton

1 *view of town, sea, hills / view of Brighton and countryside* ·
2 *£ 15 for tourists or £ 7.50 for residents / people from Brighton* ·
3 *between 1815 and 1822* · 4 *place to relax for prince / for prince to have fun / so prince could escape London* · 5 *prince's rooms, kitchen* · 6 *£ 12,30 for adults or £ 6.90 for children* · 7 *make Brighton safer and healthier* · 8 *old tunnels for dirty water / underground tunnels* · 9 *£ 12 for adults or £ 6 for children*

TRAINING SECTION: Leseverstehen ▶ S. 15–23

Reading Part 1 (Matching)

Holiday activities

1 F · 2 E · 3 D

Tipp zu A: Jack möchte mit Kindern arbeiten.

Tipp zu B: Celina sucht ein neues Betätigungsfeld.

Tipp zu C: Diese Reise ist teuer, aber Karen hat nicht viel Geld.

Tipp zu D: Celina möchte etwas Neues ausprobieren.

Tipp zu E: Zu Jack, denn August ist Ferienzeit, und er möchte die Ferien mit Kindern verbringen.

Tipp zu F: Zu Karen, denn sie möchte mit Gleichgesinnten preiswert reisen.

Reading Parts 2 and *3 (Multiple choice)

Australia's Stolen Generations

1 B · 2 A

Tipp: Das Antonym im Text zu *forced to stay* in 1 C lautet *had to leave*.

Tipp: ... *children had to leave their homes / They were given the foods ...*

Tipp: 2 C ist nicht die richtige Lösung, weil es (anders als im Text) keine verneinte Aussage ist: *They were not allowed to speak their own language* im Lesetext ist das Gegenteil von *They had to speak their own language* in 2 C.

Reading Part 1: Work practice (Matching)

1/2 B+C · 3/4 D+F · 5/6 A+E · 7/8 B+G · 9/10 A+D

Reading Part 2: Short texts (Multiple choice)

1 D · 2 B · 3 B · 4 D

Reading Part 3: Filming in New Zealand (Multiple choice)

1 A · 2 B · 3 A · 4 B · 5 B

TRAINING SECTION: Schreiben ► S. 24–31

Writing Part 1: Your photo

a) Tipp: Schlüsselwörter: *where / who / what*

b)

> I think this girl looks really funny!
> I took this photo last week in a park
> near where I live. I don't know who
> she is or what she was doing. But
> I know she was having fun.

c) Lösungsbeispiel:

Thanks! The girl is my brother's new girlfriend Laura. I took the photo last weekend. We all went swimming together and afterwards we had a picnic in the park. Laura started a competition who could look really crazy – and she won. I mean, just look at her tongue! (48 Wörter)

Writing Part 2

Eigene Erfahrungen beschreiben

a) Frage 4: Individuelle Lösungen (Notizen)

b) Blau markiert sind die Nebensätze.
Unterstrichen ist/sind
- die Verneinung von zwei Verben,
- zwei Verben im *past perfect*.

Unterkringelt ist/sind
- ein Adjektiv in der Superlativform,
- sieben Verbindungswörter *(linking words)*.

> A great weekend for me is a weekend spent outside. Last weekend, for example, I went with my friend Sam on a camping trip in the mountains. Actually, my friend Dave had wanted to come too, but he didn't have time because he had so much homework.
> We hiked along muddy valleys, we climbed steep hills and in the evening we cooked on an open fire. Although the weather was awful, it was great fun. The wet nights weren't great, but it was a wonderful feeling when I stood on the highest mountain that I had ever climbed! (98 Wörter)

Wortschatz
- Verben (im *simple past*): *went, didn't have, had, hiked, climbed, cooked, was, weren't, stood*
- Adjektive: *great, muddy, steep, open, awful, great, wet, highest*

c) Individuelle Lösungen nach dem Muster des Beispieltextes in **b)**.

Begründet Stellung beziehen

d) Markiert sind die Pro-Argumente in Hellgrau, die Kontra-Argumente in Dunkelgrau und das Ergebnis in Blau.

> As an outdoor person, I think that a weekend at home is a little bit boring. For me, getting fresh air and exercise is more relaxing than chilling on the sofa. On the other hand, if the weather is bad a weekend at home can be really nice. Moreover, sometimes my week has been so full that I just don't have the time to organize a weekend activity outside. So all in all I would say that how you spend your weekend depends on many things – the season, the weather, the time available – and there's no good or bad as long as your weekend gives you energy for the new week. (110 Wörter)

e) Individuelle Lösungen nach Muster des Beispieltextes in **d)**.

Writing Part 3: Mediation

a)
- ein Mädchen, das nur wenig Deutsch spricht und Kontakt zu Deutschen sucht
- vier Aktivitäten, bei denen Mira ihr Deutsch verbessern kann
- eine E-Mail

b)

> # Jugendzentrum Hegeda
>
> Im Jugendzentrum Hegeda können sich Jugendliche von 12 bis 18 Jahren treffen.
> Wollt ihr einfach nur eure Freunde treffen, spielen, klönen oder einfach mal entspannen, könnt ihr das bei uns tun.
>
> Euch stehen vielfältige Freizeitangebote wie zum Beispiel Tischtennis, Billard oder Tischfußball zur Verfügung sowie Kurse in Deutsch für Anfänger. Mittwochs ist von 16 Uhr bis 18 Uhr Kindercafe.
>
> Älteren Jugendlichen bieten wir Unterstützung bei der Berufsfindung, d.h. beim Bewerbungsschreiben oder bei der Lehrstellensuche.
> Und wenn ihr Stress, Kummer oder Ärger mit euren Eltern, Geschwistern oder Freunden habt, sind wir für euch da.
>
> Ihr könnt unter Anleitung Fahrräder reparieren, die Küche nutzen und euch am Kindercafe als Organisatoren beteiligen.
>
> Alle Jugendlichen von 12 bis 18 sind auch zu unseren Abenden der internationalen Küche herzlich eingeladen, an denen junge Menschen aus aller Welt die Küche ihres Landes vorstellen (3,50 Euro Kostenbeitrag). Diese Abende finden ungefähr alle zwei Wochen statt.

c)

1 *At the youth club you can meet people, you can chat and you can play games together / play and relax.*

2 *The centre also offers billiard tables, table tennis and table football.*

Tipp: weitere Vorschläge für mögliche Satzanfänge:
Facilities include … / The centre also offers activities like … / You can also play … /

3 *The centre can help you if you're looking for a job or if you need to write a letter of application / apply for a job / apply for an apprenticeship / write an application.*

4 *You can talk with somebody at the centre if you're having problems with your parents, your brothers and sisters or your boyfriend or girlfriend / if things are difficult in your family or with your friends / if you are fighting with …*

d) Lösungsbeispiel:

Dear Mira,

I have found a brochure for you. It's an advert for a youth centre where you can improve your German by meeting other kids in your free time.

At this club you can chat and you can play games together. They also offer activities like billiards, table tennis and table football. You can get help when you need to repair your bike. And you can use the kitchen – every second week the centre offers an evening of international cooking where young people cook the food of their home country for the others.

I hope this helps!

Yours

(name)

TRAINING SECTION: Sprechen ▶ S. 32–40

Sprechen – Prüfungsbeispiele

Speaking Part 1: Warming up

Prüfungsbeispiel 1

a) einsilbige Antworten, unvollständige Sätze, falsche Verbform, Sprache stockend, zu oft „äh" etc.

b) ~~I go~~ I went

Prüfungsbeispiel 2

a) informative Antworten, vollständige Sätze, abwechslungsreiche Satzkonstruktionen, flüssige und lebendige Sprechweise, benutzt *linking words* und *idioms* etc.

b) wiederholt die Frage, sagt *Well…* als Einführung

Speaking Part 2: Agreeing and disagreeing

Prüfungsbeispiel 1

a) kein guter Gesprächspartner: der Junge

b) zu kurze Antworten, keine eigenen Fragen, hält das Gespräch nicht aufrecht, zu oft „äh" etc.

Prüfungsbeispiel 2

a) informative Antworten, vollständige Sätze, abwechslungsreiche Satzkonstruktionen, flüssige und lebendige Sprechweise, halten Gespräch aufrecht, stellen Fragen, benutzen *linking words* und *idioms* etc.

b) *if you prefer, to be honest, I'm not so keen on, to tell you the truth, is that an idea?, no worries, that's a really good idea etc.*

Speaking Part 3: Describing a picture

Prüfungsbeispiel 1

a)/b) Lösungsbeispiel:

I can see a middle-aged man in a kitchen. There's a mountain of plates, cups, glasses and so on in front of him. The man has very short hair and a short beard. He is wearing a short-sleeved shirt. He looks really fed up – probably because there are so many things to wash up.

I think that the man had a party last night, and I imagine that lots of his friends came and ate and drank and had a good time. The problem is that they didn't help with the washing up, so the man has to do it alone.

I don't think he has a dishwasher because he's standing at the sink. And he isn't looking forward to this job!

The man is probably tired because he stayed up late with his friends. But I suppose he maybe feels happy because so many friends came to his party.

But one thing is certain. I wouldn't want to be him, because I hate washing up!

Speaking Part 4: Discussing a topic

Prüfungsbeispiel 1/2

a)/b)

Die Prüflinge …	Beispiel 1	Beispiel 2
… formulieren ihre Argumente und begründen sie.		✓
… lassen einander zu Wort kommen und reagieren aufeinander.	✓	✓
… bringen eigene Erfahrungen und Beispiele in die Diskussion ein.		✓
… stellen einander Fragen.		✓
… kommen zu einem gemeinsamen Ergebnis.	✓	✓

b) *Shall I start?, But on the other hand …, That's a good point., I hadn't thought of that., For this reason, I think …, So all in all …, What should be top of our list?, etc.*

Listening Part 1: Short messages

Message one: 1 A · 2 C
Message two: 3 D · 4 C

Listening Part 2: Radio ads

5 B · 6 E · 7 A · 8 C

Listening Part 3: William Shakespeare

9 *house where Shakespeare was born* · 10 *Shakespeare's old rooms and furniture* · 11 *a bit outside / about 5 kilometres away from* · 12 *600 years ago* · 13 *his/Shakespeare's mother's farm / belonged to his/Shakespeare's mother* · 14 *feed the animals/ goats, hens and pigs* · 15 *London* · 16 *1997* · 17 *a copy of Shakespeare's theatre*

Listening Part 4: Bo-Kaap, a special district in Cape Town

18 B · 19 C · 20 A · 21 A · 22 C · 23 B · 24 A · 25 B

Reading Part 1: Holiday activities

1/2 A + E · 3/4 A + G · 5/6 C + H · 7/8 B + F · 9/10 D + H

Reading Part 2: Short texts

11 B · 12 D · 13 A · 14 C · 15 B · 16 A

*Reading Part 3: High-rise living in Britain

17 D · 18 B · 19 C · 20 B · 21 D · 22 A · 23 C · 24 A · 25 D

Hinweis zu den Lösungsvorschlägen beim Schreiben:
Für die erste Schreibaufgabe (30 – 50 Wörter) werden englischsprachige Lösungsbeispiele angeboten, die als Orientierungshilfe dienen. Es sind aber natürlich auch inhaltlich andere Lösungen denkbar.
Wegen der möglichen Bandbreite an unterschiedlichen Lösungen bei den längeren Schreibaufgaben werden für diese Teilaufgaben nur die allgemeinen Aspekte knapp auf Deutsch skizziert.
Siehe dazu auch die Hinweise zur Bewertung von Inhalt und Sprache auf S. 24 sowie die Checklisten auf S. 28 und 31.

Generell gilt, dass die folgenden Punkte in deinem Text berücksichtigt sein sollten, wenn du die volle Punktzahl bekommen willst:
- Du machst wenige Wiederholungen und schweifst nicht vom Thema ab.
- Dein Text lässt sich leicht lesen.
- Dein Text ist klar formuliert und logisch aufgebaut. Du verwendest Bindewörter *(linking words)* wie *because, but, so* etc.
- Du verwendest einen vielseitigen Wortschatz und idiomatische Wendungen, z.B. *make a difference*.
- Du achtest beim Schreiben auf die Textsorte, bei einer E-Mail z.B. auf die passende Anrede und Schlussformel.
- Du bist sicher in der Verwendung verschiedener grammatischer Strukturen.
- Auch wenn bei komplizierten Sätzen vereinzelte Wortschatz- oder Grammatikfehler vorkommen, versteht man, was du sagen willst.
- Bei der Mediation übersetzt du nicht wortwörtlich, sondern gibst nur Informationen wieder, die wichtig sind.

Tipp: Zeige deinen Text einer Mitschülerin oder einem Mitschüler und lasse sie oder ihn beurteilen, ob du diese Aspekte berücksichtigt hast. Oder sprich deine Lehrerin oder deinen Lehrer an – sie können es am allerbesten beurteilen.

Writing Part 1: Your photo

Lösungsbeispiel:
Thanks! That's my cousin Carolin. She's great at skiing! I took the photo last January during a ski trip in Bavaria. It was my first time skiing and at first I was a bit scared. But Carolin taught me and on the fifth day I went down the slope alone. (50 Wörter)

Writing Part 2: Home rules

Du beginnst deinen **Blogeintrag/Online-Kommentar** mit einer kurzen, zum Thema hinführenden Einleitung und erwähnst deine eigene Haltung zum Thema (strenge bzw. zu strenge Eltern).
Im Mittelteil beantwortest du **alle** im Blogeintrag gestellten Fragen und **begründest deine Meinung mit Erfahrungen** aus deinem Familienalltag (z.B. Ausgehverbot, Hausarbeiten, Taschengeld usw.).
Schreibe am Ende einen zusammenfassenden **Ergebnissatz**.

*Writing Part 3: Mediation – Work practice

Arbeit auf einem ökologisch bewirtschafteten Bauernhof

Du beginnst deine **E-Mail** mit einer persönlichen **Anrede** *(Hello/ Dear Declan)* und sprichst deinen Leser direkt an.
In der **Einleitung** nennst du kurz das **Anliegen** deiner E-Mail (z.B. Anknüpfung an ein Gespräch, Erwähnung der Stellenausschreibung).
Im **Hauptteil** gibst du grundlegende **Informationen über den Bauernhof** (z.B. Standort, Tierhaltung, Produktion von biologischen Nahrungsmitteln usw.), nennst die **Dauer** des Praktikums (zwei Wochen) und beschreibst mindestens **vier wichtige Tätigkeiten** im Job (z.B. Hofarbeit, Tierpflege, Gartenarbeit, Verkauf von Produkten auf Bauernmärkten usw.). Außerdem nennst du die **Vor- und Nachteile** der ausgeschriebenen Stelle (z.B. Unterkunft, Essensversorgung, kostenloser Internetanschluss, keine Vergütung usw.) sowie die wichtigsten **Bewerbungsanforderungen** (Mindestalter 16 Jahre). Zuletzt skizzierst du kurz das **Bewerbungsverfahren** (Bewerbung per E-Mail).
Du beendest deine E-Mail mit einem zur Textsorte passenden **Schlusssatz** (z.B. ermunternde Worte, gute Wünsche für die Bewerbung usw.), **verabschiedest dich persönlich** *(Yours, Best wishes, Lots of love)* und unterschreibst mit deinem Namen.

Praktikum am Gerald Theater

Du beginnst deine **E-Mail** mit einer persönlichen Anrede *(Hello/Dear Declan)* und sprichst deinen Leser direkt an.

In der **Einleitung** nennst du kurz das **Anliegen** deiner E-Mail (z.B. Anknüpfung an ein Gespräch, Erwähnung der Stellenausschreibung).

Im **Hauptteil** gibst du grundlegende **Informationen über das Theater** (z.B. vielfältig, langjährige Erfahrung usw.), nennst die **Dauer** des Praktikums (zwei Wochen bis zwei Monate) und beschreibst mindestens **vier wichtige Tätigkeiten** im Job (z.B. Kostümvorbereitung, Kartenverkauf, Tontechnik, Beleuchtung, Bedienung im Café oder an der Garderobe usw.). Außerdem nennst du die **Vor- und Nachteile** der ausgeschriebenen Stelle (z.B. Freikarten, Zusammenarbeit mit professionellen Schauspielerinnen und Schauspielern, keine Vergütung usw.) sowie die wichtigsten **Bewerbungsanforderungen** (z.B. Mindestalter 15 Jahre, Bereitschaft zur Arbeit am Abend/Wochenende, Kreativität, Leidenschaft, Zuverlässigkeit usw.). Zuletzt skizzierst du kurz das **Bewerbungsverfahren** (Bewerbung per E-Mail mit Angabe des gewünschten Starttermins).

Du beendest deine E-Mail mit einem zur Textsorte passenden **Schlusssatz** (z.B. ermunternde Worte, gute Wünsche für die Bewerbung), **verabschiedest dich persönlich** *(Yours, Best wishes, Lots of Love)* und unterschreibst mit deinem Namen.

MUSTERPRÜFUNG 2 | 1. Prüfungsteil:
Hörverstehen ▶ S. 56−59

Listening Part 1: Short messages

Message one: **1** D · **2** B
Message two: **3** A · **4** D

Listening Part 2: Radio ads

5 F · **6** A · **7** B · **8** E

Listening Part 3: Three British planes

9 *1930s* · **10** *landed on water/lakes and sea / didn't need a landing strip* · **11** *took off too slowly / take off was too slow / taking off from land easier* · **12** *2nd May 1952* · **13** *world's first passenger plane/jet / first plane/jet with passengers* · **14** *crashed too often / had too many crashes / engine broke part of plane / too many unexplained crashes* · **15** *1969, 2003* · **16** *supersonic / flew faster than sound / twice as fast as sound* · **17** *carried too few passengers / couldn't carry enough passengers / too expensive to run*

Listening Part 4: Cricket in India

18 C · **19** C · **20** A · **21** C · **22** B · **23** A · **24** C · **25** B

MUSTERPRÜFUNG 2 | 2. Prüfungsteil:
Leseverstehen ▶ S. 60 − 67

Reading Part 1: Summer jobs

1/2 A + G · **3/4** E + C · **5/6** B + D · **7/8** F + H · **9/10** F + G

Reading Part 2: Short texts

11 C · **12** C · **13** A · **14** B · **15** D · **16** A

*Reading Part 3: Life in South Africa today

17 C · **18** D · **19** C · **20** A · **21** B · **22** A · **23** B · **24** A · **25** C

MUSTERPRÜFUNG 2 | 2. Prüfungsteil:
Schreiben ▶ S. 67 − 69

Hinweis zu den Lösungsvorschlägen beim Schreiben:

Für die erste Schreibaufgabe (30 − 50 Wörter) werden englischsprachige Lösungsbeispiele angeboten, die als Orientierungshilfe dienen. Es sind aber natürlich auch inhaltlich andere Lösungen denkbar.

Wegen der möglichen Bandbreite an unterschiedlichen Lösungen bei den längeren Schreibaufgaben werden für diese Teilaufgaben nur die allgemeinen Aspekte knapp auf Deutsch skizziert.

Siehe dazu auch die Hinweise zur Bewertung von Inhalt und Sprache auf S. 24 sowie die Checklisten auf S. 28 und 31.

Generell gilt, dass die folgenden Punkte in deinem Text berücksichtigt sein sollten, wenn du die volle Punktzahl bekommen willst:

- Du machst wenige Wiederholungen und schweifst nicht vom Thema ab.
- Dein Text lässt sich leicht lesen.
- Dein Text ist klar formuliert und logisch aufgebaut. Du verwendest Bindewörter *(linking words)* wie *because, but, so* etc.
- Du verwendest einen vielseitigen Wortschatz und idiomatische Wendungen, z.B. *make a difference*.
- Du achtest beim Schreiben auf die Textsorte, bei einer E-Mail z.B. auf die passende Anrede und Schlussformel.
- Du bist sicher in der Verwendung verschiedener grammatischer Strukturen.
- Auch wenn bei komplizierten Sätzen vereinzelte Wortschatz- oder Grammatikfehler vorkommen, versteht man, was du sagen willst.
- Bei der Mediation übersetzt du nicht wortwörtlich, sondern gibst nur Informationen wieder, die wichtig sind.

Tipp: Zeige deinen Text einer Mitschülerin oder einem Mitschüler und lasse sie oder ihn beurteilen, ob du diese Aspekte berücksichtigt hast. Oder sprich deine Lehrerin oder deinen Lehrer an − sie können es am allerbesten beurteilen.

Writing Part 1: Your photo

Lösungsbeispiel:
That's my friend Noah. He just passed his driving test, so we decided to celebrate with a huge ice cream. Just the perfect thing to do on a hot day like this! Noah invited me and I got five different flavours: strawberry, vanilla, chocolate, cookies and mango. Hungry? (48 Wörter)

Writing Part 2: How fit are you?

Du beginnst deinen **Blogeintrag/Online-Kommentar** mit einer kurzen zum Thema hinführenden Einleitung und erwähnst deine **eigene Haltung** zum Thema (Sport als Hobby oder Pflicht). Im Mittelteil beantwortest du **alle** im Blogeintrag gestellten Fragen und **begründest deine Meinung mit Erfahrungen** aus deinem Alltag (z.B. wie regelmäßig du Sport treibst, ob du Spaß daran hast usw.).
Schreibe am Ende einen zusammenfassenden Ergebnissatz.

*Writing Part 3: Mediation – A warm welcome

Lichtblick – Kontakt und Beratungsstellen

Du beginnst deine **E-Mail** mit einer persönlichen Anrede *(Hello/Dear Adnan)* und sprichst deinen Leser direkt an.
In der **Einleitung** nennst du kurz das **Anliegen** deiner E-Mail (z.B. Anknüpfung an ein Gespräch, Erwähnung der Broschüre). Im **Hauptteil** nennst du den Zweck der beworbenen Einrichtung (Beratung für Menschen unterschiedlicher Herkunft). Du gibst **mindestens vier wichtige Angebote** des Vereins wieder (z.B. soziale Veranstaltungen, Beratung für Menschen mit Migrationshintergrund, Spielgruppen für Kinder, psychologische Unterstützung usw.) und schilderst die **wichtigsten Informationen zur Organisation** (z.B. Standorte, Öffnungszeiten, Möglichkeiten zur Kontaktaufnahme usw.).
Du beendest deine E-Mail mit einem zur Textsorte passenden **Schlusssatz** (z.B. ermunternde Worte, gute Wünsche für die Zukunft usw.), **verabschiedest dich persönlich** *(Yours, Best wishes, Lots of Love)* und unterschreibst mit deinem Namen.

Sport im Park

Du beginnst deine **E-Mail** mit einer persönlichen Anrede *(Hello/Dear Adnan)* und sprichst deinen Leser direkt an.
In der **Einleitung** nennst du kurz das **Anliegen** deiner E-Mail (z.B. Anknüpfung an ein Gespräch, Erwähnung der Anzeige). Im **Hauptteil** nennst du den Zweck der beworbenen Einrichtung (Sportverein für junge Menschen). Du nennst **mindestens vier wichtige Informationen über den Verein** (z.B. Zielgruppe, Programmangebot, Kosten, Ausstattung usw.) und schilderst die **wichtigsten Informationen zur Organisation** (z.B. Standort, Treffzeiten, Registrierungsverfahren usw.).
Du beendest deine E-Mail mit einem zur Textsorte passenden **Schlusssatz** (z.B. ermunternde Worte, gute Wünsche usw.), **verabschiedest dich persönlich** *(Yours, Best wishes, Lots of love)* und unterschreibst mit deinem Namen.

Prüfungsbeispiel 2

 Das zweite Prüfungsbeispiel ist **ein gutes Beispiel**. Höre zu und bearbeite die Aufgaben.

a) Was machen die beiden Prüflinge gut? Notiere mindestens drei positive Aspekte.

b) Höre mindestens drei gute Formulierungen heraus, die du bei der Prüfung eventuell selber verwenden könntest.

Speaking Part 3: Describing a picture

Prüfungsbeispiel 1

 Das erste Prüfungsbeispiel ist **verbesserungsfähig**. Höre zu und bearbeite die Aufgaben.

a) Betrachte das Bild und lies die Aufgabenstellung in der Sprechblase. Dann höre dir die Bildbeschreibung des Prüflings an.

> Talk about the picture.
> What can you see?
> What do you think the man
> is feeling?

b) Die Bildbeschreibung des Prüflings ist nicht schlecht, aber du kannst sie verbessern. Beantworte die Fragen in den Sprechblasen und formuliere die Sätze neu. Nutze dafür den Platz auf Seite 38.

> What does he look like?

> Can you link the first two sentences?

> Another word for "lots of"?

> Where are the plates, cups, etc.?

> Do you think he has a dishwasher? Why not?

> What happened at the party? Lots of friends came and ... ?

> Would you like to be with him? Why (not)?

> Why?

I can see a man.
He is in a kitchen.
There are lots of plates, cups, glasses and so on.
I think that the man had a party last night. But his friends didn't help with the washing up.
The man is probably tired.
But I suppose he maybe feels happy because so many friends came to his party.

_____

_____

_____

_____

_____

_____

Prüfungsbeispiel 2

14
Das zweite Prüfungsbeispiel zum gleichen Bild ist **deutlich besser**.
Höre zu und vergleiche deine Sätze aus **1b).** Hast du Ähnliches geschrieben?

Tipp

Deine Sätze müssen natürlich nicht identisch sein. Vielleicht hattest du ganz andere Ideen, die genauso gut sind – oder noch besser!

Speaking Part 4: Discussing a topic

Prüfungsbeispiel 1

a) Lies die Aufgabenstellung in der Sprechblase und betrachte die Bilder, die den Prüflingen vorlagen.

> *You both have pictures which show where people do their shopping.*
> *Now please talk together about the pros and cons of out-of-town shopping centres,*
> *local shops and online shopping. What do you prefer? What are the consequences for towns,*
> *cities and local shop owners?*

b) Lies nun die Sätze in der Tabelle. Dann höre dir das erste Prüfungsbeispiel an und setze in der Spalte
15   für Beispiel 1 ein Häkchen, wenn der Satz zutrifft.

Die Prüflinge ...	Beispiel 1	Beispiel 2
... formulieren ihre Argumente und begründen sie.		
... lassen einander zu Wort kommen und reagieren aufeinander.		
... bringen eigene Erfahrungen und Beispiele in die Diskussion ein.		
... stellen einander Fragen.		
... kommen zu einem gemeinsamen Ergebnis.		

Prüfungsbeispiel 2

a) Nun höre dir das zweite Prüfungsbeispiel an und setze in der Spalte für Beispiel 2 ein Häkchen, wenn der Satz zutrifft.

b) Höre mindestens drei gute Formulierungen heraus, die du bei der Prüfung eventuell selber verwenden könntest.

4. Sprechen – *Now you*

Hier hast du die Möglichkeit, die Strategien, die du auf den letzten Seiten kennen gelernt hast, bei ausgewählten Aufgaben umzusetzen und zu üben. Arbeite mit einem Partner oder einer Partnerin zusammen.

Speaking Part 1: Warming up

a) Stelle deinem Partner oder deiner Partnerin fünf Fragen.
b) Beantworte dann fünf Fragen deines Partners oder deiner Partnerin.

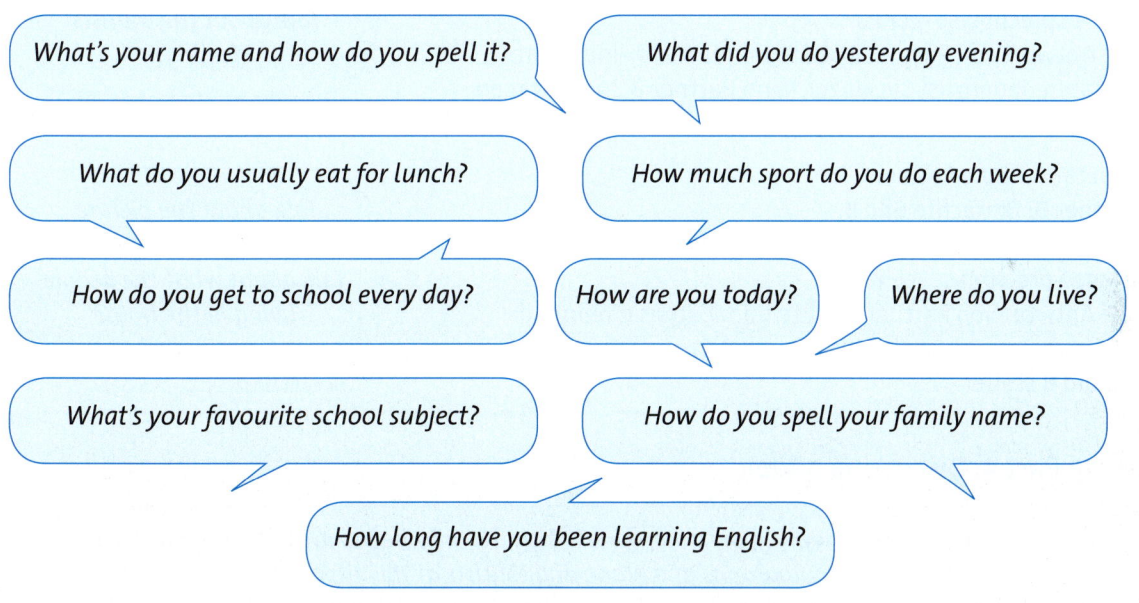

What's your name and how do you spell it?

What did you do yesterday evening?

What do you usually eat for lunch?

How much sport do you do each week?

How do you get to school every day?

How are you today?

Where do you live?

What's your favourite school subject?

How do you spell your family name?

How long have you been learning English?

Speaking Part 2: Agreeing and disagreeing

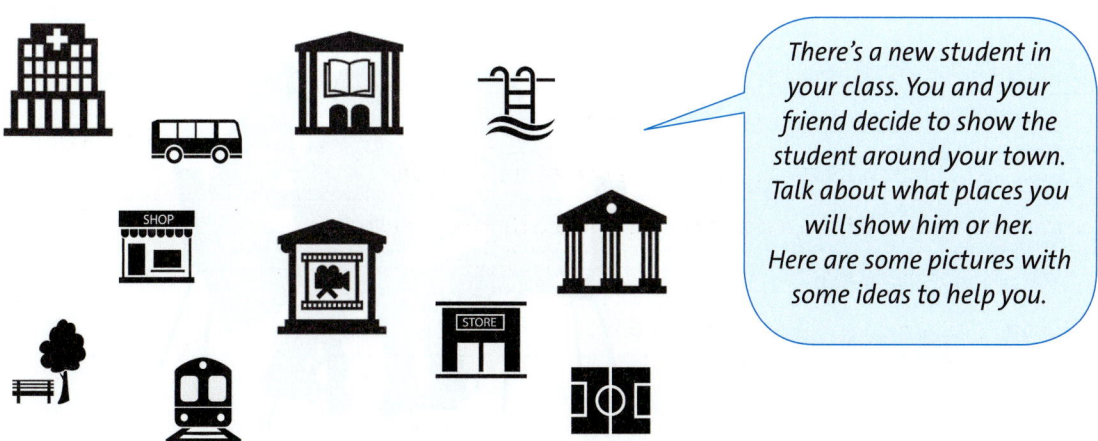

There's a new student in your class. You and your friend decide to show the student around your town. Talk about what places you will show him or her. Here are some pictures with some ideas to help you.

Speaking Part 3: Describing a picture

Zusatzfragen zu Bild A:
- What are the tourists doing?
- Where are they going?
- Have you ever flown before?

Zusatzfragen zu Bild B:
- Why is it noisy?
- Is your house or flat quiet?
- Would you like to live in this house?

a) Ihr habt keine Vorbereitungszeit!
Partner A: Betrachte **Bild A**.
Partner B: Übernimm die Rolle des Prüfers
(siehe Sprechblase rechts):
Die Antwort von Partner A sollte mindestens eineinhalb
Minuten dauern. Ist sie kürzer, kann Partner B Zusatzfragen
zu **Bild A** stellen.

> *Talk about the picture.*
> *What can you see?*
> *Talk about the tourists'*
> *feelings.*

b) Nun tauscht die Rollen:
Partner B: Betrachte **Bild B**.
Partner A: Übernimm die Rolle der Prüferin
(siehe Sprechblase rechts):
Die Antwort von Partner B sollte mindestens eineinhalb
Minuten dauern. Ist sie kürzer, kann Partner A Zusatzfragen
zu **Bild B** stellen.

> *Talk about the picture.*
> *What can you see?*
> *Talk about what the people*
> *living in the house*
> *are feeling.*

Speaking Part 4: Discussing a topic

> *There are plans to build a new airport or terminal about ten kilometres away from your school.*
> *Look at your photographs of a plane and tourists at the airport again.*
> *Now I'd like you to talk together about airports and flying. What are the advantages and*
> *disadvantages? Should airports be close to towns or cities? How important is flying to you?*
> *What about the economy and the environment?*

MUSTERPRÜFUNG 1

Schriftliche Prüfung, Teil I: Hörverstehen `Berlin` `Brandenburg`

Listening Part 1: Short messages

_____ / 4

17

- *You are going to hear two short messages.*
- *You will hear the recording twice.*
- *There are four questions in this part, two questions for each message.*
- *Look at the pictures and then listen to the recording.*
- *Choose the correct picture and put a tick (✓) in the right box.*

Message one

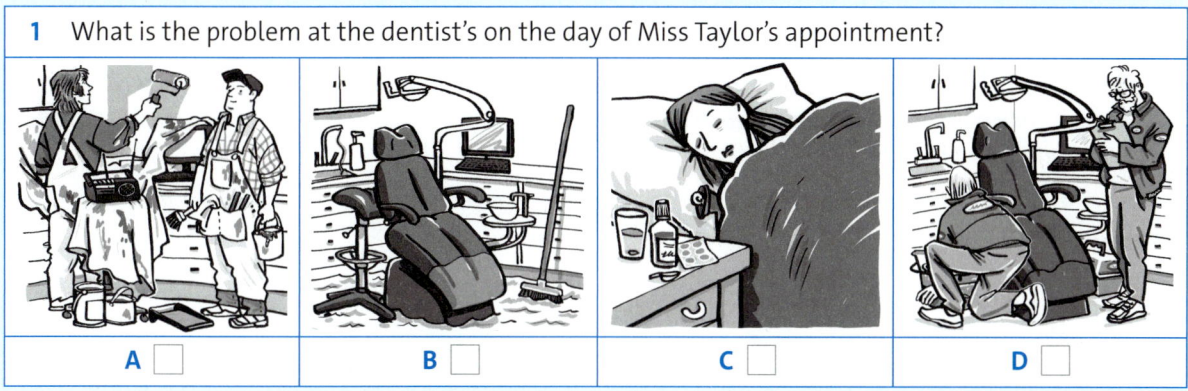

1 What is the problem at the dentist's on the day of Miss Taylor's appointment?

A ☐   B ☐   C ☐   D ☐

2 When is Miss Taylor's new appointment at the dentist's?

A ☐   B ☐   C ☐   D ☐

Message two

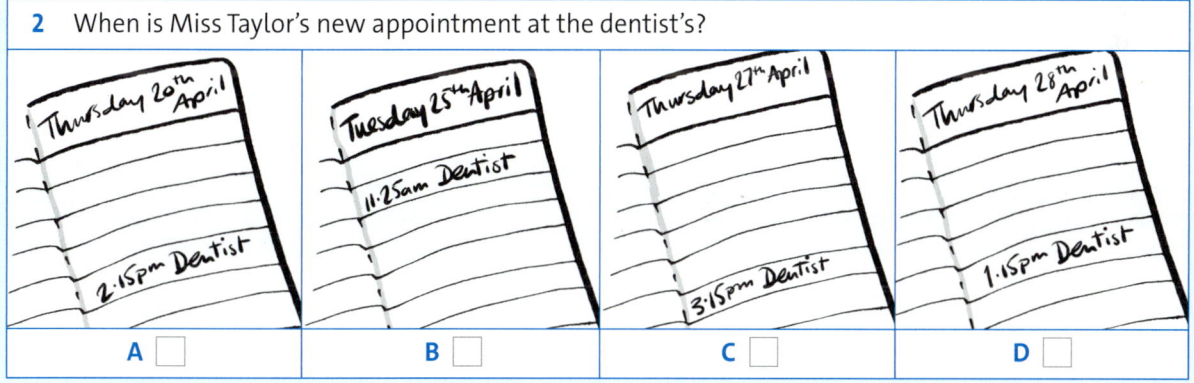

3 Hassan has asked the way to the post office. Which way should he go?

A ☐   B ☐   C ☐   D ☐

41

4 In what sort of a road is the post office?

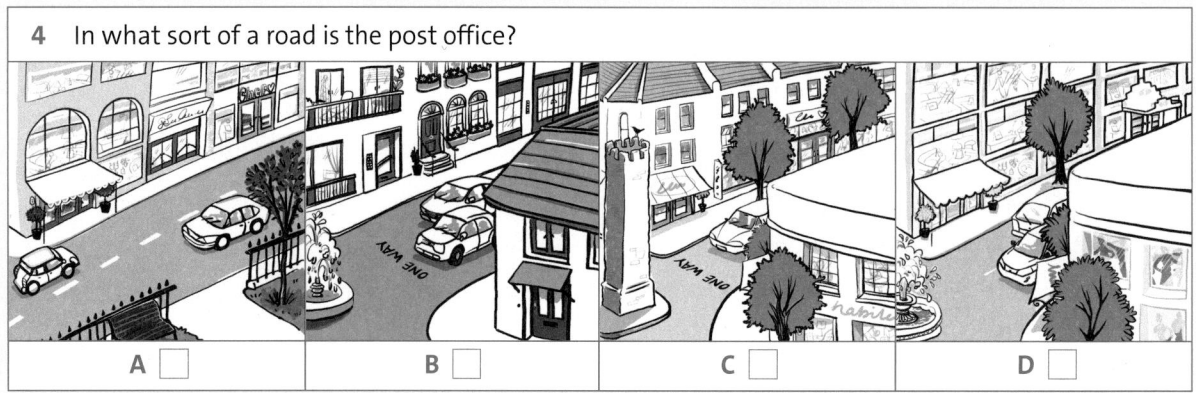

| A ☐ | B ☐ | C ☐ | D ☐ |

Listening Part 2: Radio ads   _____ / 4

18

- *Please note: You do not need to understand every word to do this task.*
- *You are going to hear four radio ads.*
- *You will hear the recording twice.*
- *Read the slogans below first, then listen to the recording.*
- *For each ad choose the correct slogan from the list (A–F) and put a tick (✓) in the right box.*
- *There is only one correct slogan for each ad.*
- *Two slogans can't be matched.*

A Sign up for a course.

B A career change.

C Dispose of your rubbish responsibly.

D Live more healthily.

E Always put on your seat belts.

F Travel by bus.

		Slogan					
Number	Radio ads	A	B	C	D	E	F
5	Radio ad 1	☐	☐	☐	☐	☐	☐
6	Radio ad 2	☐	☐	☐	☐	☐	☐
7	Radio ad 3	☐	☐	☐	☐	☐	☐
8	Radio ad 4	☐	☐	☐	☐	☐	☐

Listening Part 3: William Shakespeare

_____ / 9

19

- *You are going to hear a presentation about William Shakespeare.*
- *You will hear the recording twice.*
- *Complete the table below. Use 1 to 5 words or numbers.*

Name of building	Where is it?	When was it built?	What is its link with William Shakespeare?	What can tourists see or do here?
House in Henley Street	*Stratford-upon-Avon*	✕	**9** _____ _____	**10** See: _____ _____
Mary Arden's Farm	**11** _____ Stratford-upon-Avon	**12** _____ _____	**13** _____ _____	**14** Do: _____ _____
Globe Theatre	**15** _____ _____	**16** _____ _____	✕	**17** See: _____ _____

*Listening Part 4: Bo-Kaap, a special district in Cape Town

_____ / 8

20

- *You are going to hear a radio travel report by three students who visited Cape Town in South Africa.*
- *You will hear the recording twice.*
- *Read the statements below first, then listen to the recording.*
- *Put a tick (✓) in the box next to the correct statement.*
- *Only one statement is correct in each case.*

A street in Bo-Kaap

18 The Auwal mosque in Bo-Kaap was built	A	☐	a hundred years ago.
	B	☐	at the end of the 18th century.
	C	☐	in 1974.

19 The people who ruled Cape Town back then	A	☐	were Asian.
	B	☐	built the Auwal mosque.
	C	☐	were Europeans.

20 The Asian workers who worked outside of Cape Town worked in	A	☐	sugar fields.
	B	☐	gold mines.
	C	☐	factories.

21 Katie found the information in the Bo-Kaap Museum	A	☐	shocking.
	B	☐	surprising.
	C	☐	amusing.

22 Alfie was impressed by	A	☐	the wonderful furniture that Asian worker families used to have.
	B	☐	how the Bo-Kaap museum building was built.
	C	☐	both A + B

23 What is so special in this part of Wale Street is that	A	☐	mostly Asian people live there.
	B	☐	the houses are brightly painted.
	C	☐	the people speak so many different languages.

24 Wale Street today is an example of how people in South Africa	A	☐	are mixing more than they did before.
	B	☐	have more money than before.
	C	☐	have moved away from the narrow streets of city centres.

25 Haroun felt that as a result of recent developments in Bo-Kaap	A	☐	tourists should no longer visit Cape Town.
	B	☐	people don't know their neighbours as well as they did before.
	C	☐	both A + B

Schriftliche Prüfung, Teil II: Leseverstehen/Schreiben `Berlin`

Reading Part 1: Holiday activities

_____ / 10

- *These teenagers (a–e) want to do some activities in their holidays.*
- *First read the information about these teens on page 45, then look at the descriptions of the activities (A–G) on page 46.*
- *In each case find the **two** activities the teens would like to do. Write the letters of the activities in the boxes next to the teenagers' names.*
- *Some of the activities can be chosen more than once.*

No.	Activity 1	Activity 2	The teenagers
1/2			**a) Harry** loves to spend his holidays at the seaside or in the mountains. He loves canyoning, a sport in which you make your way down a narrow rocky gorge, sometimes jumping from rock to rock, sometimes wading through the water or even swimming in it. And he loves riding his 24-gear, front and rear suspension mountain bike. He loves the challenge of rough mountain trails – the rougher and steeper, the better. And he doesn't mind carrying his bike over the rougher bits if necessary.
3/4			**b) Rosanna** loves all water sports. She has won swimming competitions, and has done courses in canoeing and kayaking. Now she is looking for a new water sport challenge – something she has never done before. Ideally it would be based in the south-west of England, so that she can combine her activity holiday with a visit to her cousins in Plymouth.
5/6			**c) Ahn** has always loved swimming and being in water. Back stroke, breast stroke, crawl – he is a master of them all. And still he wants to improve his swimming skills, for example his butterfly style. If he can progress enough, who knows, maybe one day he'll become a swimming coach, or even compete in Team GB? Fitness is very important to Ahn. He also likes to cycle in order to keep fit, but unfortunately his bike got stolen recently.
7/8			**d) Yvonne** was 5 when she first learned to ride a bike and she has never looked back. She loves feeling the wind in her hair and seeing the countryside while pedaling hard through it. She'll happily carry a tent and other heavy equipment in her panniers, so she prefers to avoid steep climbs. Sometimes she dreams of trying out a bike with an electric motor or some other form of power supply, but she has still never done it.
9/10			**e) Steve** adores his lightweight drop-handlebar racing bike – it's his pride and joy. He is a member of a cycling team and has done well in cycle races in a number of local competitions. His ambition is to take part in an international competition such as the *Tour de Yorkshire*, and he is willing to put in the necessary hours of training. He also likes sports like rowing and canoeing, but now finds lakes and rivers a bit tame. He is looking for a new boating challenge.

A Coasteering is the new fun sport that combines the best of the sea with the best of the mountains. Wearing wetsuits to keep warm and helmets to keep safe, we use rocky north Devon as our play-ground. We scramble over rocks, walk through water, and do cliff jumps into the sea – jumps of 10 metres or more! It's so much fun that sometimes, if we're lucky, even the seals come and join us!

B Do you like your cycling to be a little smoother? Then join us on long-distance cycling trips on the Transpennine Trail, the Tissington Trail and other routes that make use of old railway lines. These trails avoid the hills by using old railway bridges and tunnels. We do both day and weekend trips.

C Swim UK organizes courses for all levels. We help complete beginners to overcome their fears and help experienced swimmers to develop and maximize their skills. And we also offer specialist courses for divers, life savers and those wishing to become swimming teachers. We run courses at pools all over the country – there's probably one near you!

D Come sea kayaking in the beautiful south-west of England! Based near Plymouth, we were founded over 15 years ago and we know every inch of the area, which is probably one of the best in the UK for sea kayaking. We offer day expeditions, 3-day expeditions and 10-day expeditions for every ability, and provide quality equipment including lightweight paddles, dry bags for personal belongings and either one-piece paddle suits or cags and trousers, as you prefer. Alternatively, you are welcome to use your own equipment.

E If you're into all-terrain off-roading, we have just the right circuits for you – from gentle slopes to strenuous climbs and dizzying descents, from purpose-made off-road cycling tracks to circuits that take you over rocks, through rivers and swamps. Bring your own bike or hire one from us.

F Enjoy riding a bike? Then why not upgrade to motorcycling to get the most out of those steep climbs? We can train you to ride any size of bike or scooter. We offer training courses for all levels, beginning with the Compulsory Basic Training (CBT test) which you must complete by law before biking on your own. Don't think of it as a driving test – the CBT can be good fun, and you may even make a friend or two on the course!

G Whether you are experienced or completely new to surfing, a course at our Surf School at Polzeath in Cornwall will allow you to make maximum progress in the time that you have available. We'll teach you all the basic surfing techniques, water safety and other surfing knowledge that you'll need to enjoy surfing safely. Three and five-day courses available.

H The 6,000-seat velodrome where British cyclists won gold at the London 2012 Olympic Games is the fastest track in the world – and it's open for you! Everyone can cycle here, and you don't even need a bike – you can hire everything you need. We can teach you the art of speed cycling, or if you're more ambitious, why not register for our four-day professional cyclist course?

Reading Part 2: Short texts

_____ / 6

- Look at the text and the statements in each task.
- Put a tick (✓) next to the statement that matches the text – A, B, C or D.
- There is only one correct statement for each sign.

11

A	☐	Be very careful when you walk past this sign.
B	☐	Go no further: you could die in the water.
C	☐	The cliffs are dangerous and you could be killed if you fall onto the rocks.
D	☐	You mustn't go past this notice if you are scared of heights.

If you find a cat, please
- feed it, offer it a bowl of fresh water (many cats are allergic to milk) and give it shelter

and either
- call or email *Cats Protection*, the charity that helps over 140 000 cats each year

or
- post "cat found" notices around your neighbourhood.
- If you still can't find an owner for the cat, please take it to a vet who can check if it is wearing a microchip. If it is, the microchip will allow you to identify the cat's owner. There is no charge for this service.

12 If you find a cat you should

A	☐	give it food and some milk, and keep it.
B	☐	take it immediately to the Cats Protection charity.
C	☐	pay for a vet to look for a micro-chip.
D	☐	take it into your house or make a home for it outside temporarily.

Monica House Nursery is here to help busy parents with their children. Our capacity is for up to 25 children and we welcome both newborn babies and toddlers up to the age of 3.

We have an enviable reputation for providing a warm and friendly atmosphere in which your child can learn through play.

All facilities fully baby-proofed. Open Monday to Friday 6.30 am to 8.30 pm (term time only).

Please do not hesitate to contact us.

Phone: 01394 269021

Email: **enquiries@monicahouse.co.uk**

13   The Monica House Nursery

A		accepts all children aged three years or less.
B		is a place where mothers can play with their children.
C		has a good reputation because its rooms are baby-proofed.
D		can look after a two-week-old child during the summer holidays.

GP Crash Driving Courses

Getting your license can take about a year– but take one of our crash driving courses and you could have your driving license by the end of the week!

With our *Pass in a Week* course, you'll be driving six hours a day and you'll take your test on the sixth day. The fee for the course includes the registration fee for your driving test.

Note: the normal waiting time for a driving test is 6 – 8 weeks if you book it yourself, but we guarantee you an appointment for a test within six days of starting your course.

For more information, please call Gary on: 05923 672 071

14

A		Learning to drive with a GP Crash Driving Course often takes about a year.
B		You pay for the *Pass in a Week* course and pay for the driving test in addition.
C		Take a GP Crash Course, and the wait for the driving test is shorter than otherwise.
D		With the *Pass in a Week* course you must book the driving test by yourself.

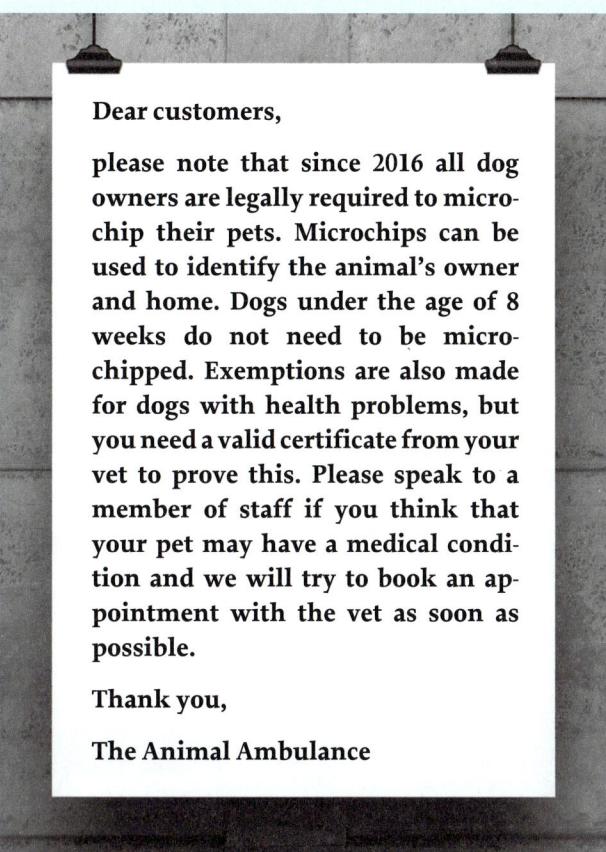

Dear customers,

please note that since 2016 all dog owners are legally required to microchip their pets. Microchips can be used to identify the animal's owner and home. Dogs under the age of 8 weeks do not need to be microchipped. Exemptions are also made for dogs with health problems, but you need a valid certificate from your vet to prove this. Please speak to a member of staff if you think that your pet may have a medical condition and we will try to book an appointment with the vet as soon as possible.

Thank you,

The Animal Ambulance

15

A	☐	Since 2016, it is the responsibility of the vet to microchip your dog.
B	☐	An eight-week old dog is required by law to carry a microchip.
C	☐	If you think your dog has health problems you don't have to worry about microchipping it.
D	☐	The Animal Ambulance can only microchip dogs that are less than 8 weeks old.

KCS - Kevin's Cleaning Services

I will happily do your cleaning for you, from the daily washing up, hoovering and tidying to thorough cleaning of your kitchen (including all appliances), bathroom and toilets.
And to give you peace of mind, the first clean will be completely free if you book a weekly service.
I really enjoy my work and have a reputation among friends, family and long-standing customers for my excellent work.
I charge £9 per hour.

Reduced charge for weekly bookings.

Kevin's Cleaning Services 00793552475
Kevin's Cleaning Services 00793552475
Kevin's Cleaning Services 00793552475
Kevin's Cleaning Services 00793552475
Kevin's Cleaning Services 00793552475
Kevin's Cleaning Services 00793552475

16

A	☐	Kevin helps you with your household chores.
B	☐	Kevin will clean the kitchen floor, but not the oven, fridge, microwave, etc.
C	☐	So far Kevin has worked for friends and family only.
D	☐	You pay less if you ask Kevin to clean your house every two weeks.

* Reading Part 3: High-rise living in Britain

_____ / 9

- *Read the text and the statements on page 51.*
- *Put a tick (✓) in the box next to the correct answer.*
- *Only one answer is correct in each case.*

High-rise apartment blocks have long had a bad press in Britain. People think of the 1960s tower blocks that were usually built for people in lower-paid jobs. The flats were small and the
5 entrances were dark and dirty, full of litter and graffiti. The lifts kept breaking down. That was no joke if you lived on the 10th floor and arrived home with your week's shopping or a child in a wheelchair. The general view was that people
10 only lived in such buildings if they had no alternative. In several cities, councils destroyed some of their high-rise apartment blocks.

Of course, the tower blocks have always had their fans, above all because of the amazing
15 views that residents often have from their flats. In addition, people in tower blocks often say that they feel safer than in a house. That's because nobody can climb through the window of a flat on the 16th floor: in fact, nobody can even
20 look in, so you don't have to draw your curtains at night. And the flats are largely free from mice, ants and spiders. These voices, however, were long in the minority. Not any more.

Look at the skyline of most British cities to-
25 day and you'll see that apartment blocks are going up all around you. Why this sudden popularity of flats? One reason is that with land becoming more and more expensive, houses are simply costing too much for many people. Build-
30 ing taller, it seems, is the only way of building cheaper homes. And the new trend for flats also reflects a change in lifestyle. In the past, a house with a garden was seen as an ideal, but these days many people get home late from work, so
35 they have no time for garden work. Instead, they prefer to have a few plants on an easily-managed balcony.

What's more, the apartments that have been built in the last few years attract people on
40 good incomes. CCTV cameras keep the entrances safe, and companies are employed to clean the corridors and maintain the lifts. Some of the modern flats are built as 'pods' – that is to say, each flat is built as a self-contained unit, with
45 bathrooms and kitchen equipped to a high standard, and the pods are then simply placed one on top of the other. This is often less costly

Tower block in London

than traditional building techniques, and customers can make their choice of equipment as they would do if they were buying a car. 50

It is true that families with children still usually prefer to live in a house with a front door, a back door and a garden. Parents can keep an eye on their children, and it's often easier to get to know your neighbours by chatting over 55 the garden fence than by sharing the lift up to the 8th floor. But a recent report has challenged the widely-held view that high-rise blocks offer a less healthy living environment.

Experts from the University of Bern in Swit- 60 zerland found that people who live on the 8th floor or above are likely to live longer than those who live on the lower floors. Those living higher up, they claim, are 40% less likely to die of lung disease, and 35% less likely to die from heart dis- 65 ease – partly because walking up more stairs keeps people fitter. There is also less air pollution on the higher floors and people are also less affected by traffic noise.

The British population is expected to grow 70 from about 65 million in 2016 to 75 million by 2040, so millions of new homes will have to be built. If we want to protect our countryside, we will have to build them in our cities, and as the price of land in cities goes up, it is clear that 75 more people will have to live in flats. The apartment blocks being built today are here to stay.

17	A	☐	were often not very attractive.
The flats in the 1960s tower blocks	B	☐	were not always clean, but at least had good lifts.
	C	☐	were for poor families.
	D	☐	both A + C

18	A	☐	full of insects.
Some people today feel that tower block flats are	B	☐	safer because burglars cannot break in so easily.
	C	☐	dangerous because you could fall out of the windows.
	D	☐	too dark when the curtains are closed at night.

19	A	☐	people have more money, so they can pay the higher rents.
Flats are becoming more popular again because	B	☐	people want to live higher off the ground floor.
	C	☐	they are easier to take care of.
	D	☐	they sometimes have a nice garden.

20	A	☐	are protected by CCTV cameras.
More and more of the flats now	B	☐	are better quality than those built in the 1960s.
	C	☐	are built exclusively for rich people.
	D	☐	all of them (A + B + C)

21	A	☐	can only meet other residents in the lift.
People in these modern high-rise flats	B	☐	can't see who comes in and out of their building.
	C	☐	don't have to pay anything for the extra facilities.
	D	☐	don't need to worry about cleaning the communal areas.

22	A	☐	are often cheaper than other flats.
The flats that are built as pods	B	☐	have poor quality kitchens and bathrooms.
	C	☐	can only be used at ground floor level.
	D	☐	all look exactly the same on the inside.

23	A	☐	now want to live in a nice modern flat.
The text argues that most British families	B	☐	like to meet their neighbours in the garden.
	C	☐	think that living in a house is better for their children.
	D	☐	don't like to share the lift with other people.

24	A	☐	helps against heart disease.
According to a recent report, living on higher floors in apartment blocks	B	☐	is dangerous because the air is very dirty.
	C	☐	is louder than living on the lower floors.
	D	☐	both A + B

25 The writer says that more British people will have to live in flats in the future because	A	☐	the population is rising too quickly.
	B	☐	too many new homes have already been built.
	C	☐	fewer people want to live in the countryside.
	D	☐	land is becoming more expensive.

Schriftliche Prüfung, Teil II: Leseverstehen/Schreiben `Berlin`

Writing Part 1: Your photo

_____ / 5

- *You have posted this photo.*
- *Your friend Oliver wants to know more.*
- *Answer his questions.*
- *Write 30–50 words.*

I like your photo!
Who is that?
When was this?
Where did you take the photo?

Writing Part 2: Home rules

Inhalt: _____ / 6   Sprache: _____ / 6

- *Read what a blogger has written below.*
- *Then write back, answering all of his questions.*
- *Write a minimum of 100 words.*

www.teens4teens.co.uk

Name:
Homeboy52

My parents have always been quite strict. In our house there are rules that my sister and I have to obey. Even now (I'm 16) I have to message my mum or dad every hour when I'm out of the house so that they know I'm safe. And I have to be home by nine o'clock in the evening.

So I'd like to know how it is in your home. Do you think your parents are strict or even too strict? What are you allowed to do (weekends, evenings, ...) – and what are you not allowed to do? What happens when you break a rule? And last but not least: how strict do you think parents should be?

*Writing Part 3: Mediation – Work practice

_____ / 8

Your English friend Declan is interested in doing a two-week internship in Germany.
He has found an offer on the internet and asked you to help him understand the programme.

- *Read the two internship offers.*
- *Choose **one** offer.*
- *Write an email to Declan telling him about the internship.*
- *Say what the work is and mention at least four important aspects of the job.*
- ***Do not translate word for word**, just give the main information.*
- *Write complete sentences.*

www.biomiohof.de

Arbeit auf einem ökologisch bewirtschafteten Bauernhof

Interessierst du dich für die Tierpflege und für die Arbeit auf dem Land?

Wir suchen dringend Hilfe auf unserem kleinen Bauernhof zwischen Celle und Wolfsburg. Auf einer überschaubaren Fläche von zwei Hektar (20.000 m²) züchten wir ca. 200 Hühner, 10 bis 15 Ziegen sowie Honigbienen. Wir produzieren unseren eigenen biologischen Honig und Ziegenkäse und verkaufen ca. 4.000 Bioeier im Monat.

Während eines zweiwöchigen Praktikums bei uns kannst du dich an der Tierpflege beteiligen sowie bei der Hofarbeit anpacken. Dazu gehören neben der normalen Gartenarbeit (Hecken schneiden, Pflanzen und Bäume gießen, Müll entsorgen) auch leichte Bauarbeiten (z.B. Zäune und Hütten reparieren). An Wochenenden darfst du uns auf regionale Wochenmärkte begleiten, um dort unsere Ware zu verkaufen. Somit erhältst du einen echten Einblick in das

Leben von Kleinbauern und in die Realität der heutigen ökologischen Landwirtschaft.

Das Praktikum wird nicht vergütet. Dafür bieten wir dir eine komfortable Unterkunft an, entweder in einem unserer Gästezimmer oder in einem beheizten Wohnwagen. Beide Wohngelegenheiten sind mit guten Betten, sauberer Bettwäsche, Badezimmer mit Toilette, Badewanne und Handtüchern komplett ausgestattet. Dazu bereiten wir jeden Tag zwei warme Mahlzeiten vor (ausschließlich Bio-Zutaten) und stellen Pausenbrote und Getränke zur Verfügung. Gelegentlich veranstalten wir auch gemeinsame Backrunden, um unsere eigenen biologischen Produkte zu verarbeiten und zu genießen!
Waschmaschine, kostenfreies W-LAN / Internetzugang vorhanden.

Interessenten müssen mindestens 16 Jahre alt sein. Bitte schick deine Bewerbung per E-Mail an info@biomiohof.de.

Wir freuen uns auf deine Anfrage und antworten schnellstmöglich.

www.geraldtheater.de/praktikum

Praktikum am Gerald Theater

Das Gerald Theater bietet Praktika mit vielfältigen Tätigkeiten, die einen umfassenden Einblick in die Welt des Theaters vermitteln. Wir sind ständig auf der Suche nach angehenden Schauspielern oder Schauspielerinnen sowie engagierten Mitarbeitern für die Ton- und Beleuchtungstechnik. Als Praktikant hilfst du außerdem bei der Vorbereitung von Kostümen, in der Schneiderei, bei der Arbeit am Bühnenbild sowie im Marketing und Kartenvertrieb mit und bedienst im Café, an der Garderobe etc.

Wir sind ein engagiertes, erfahrenes Team und du erhältst bei uns fundierte Einblicke in den künstlerischen Entstehungsprozess einer Inszenierung. Theatererfahrung ist kein Muss! Vielmehr interessiert uns deine Kreativität, Flexibilität und natürlich deine Leidenschaft für Schauspiel und Theater. Wir erwarten eine selbstständige Arbeitsweise und die Bereitschaft zu unregelmäßigen Arbeitszeiten. Arbeit am Abend und am Wochenende kann verlangt werden, aber ein Maximum von 35 Stunden in der Woche wird nicht überschritten.

Ein Gehalt können wir dir leider nicht zahlen, aber du wirst dafür intensiv und konstruktiv betreut und bekommst die einmalige Gelegenheit, eng mit professionellen Schauspielern und Schauspielerinnen zusammenzuarbeiten. Außerdem erhältst du Freikarten für alle Produktionen im Gerald Theater.

Grundsätzlich müssen Praktikanten im Gerald Theater mindestens 15 Jahre alt sein. Praktika sind normalerweise zwei Wochen lang, können jedoch nach Absprache auf maximal zwei Monate verlängert werden.

Bitte teile uns mit, wann du anfangen möchtest, und schicke deine aussagekräftige Bewerbung per E-Mail an: praktikum@geraldtheater.de.

Mündliche Prüfung

Speaking Part 1: Warming up Berlin Brandenburg

Answer these questions about yourself.

Hello. How are you feeling today?

Can you tell me your name, please and how you spell it?

Do you have any pets?

And do you play any instrument?

What's your favourite subject at school?

What do you normally eat for breakfast?

Speaking Part 2: Agreeing and disagreeing `Berlin`

> *I'm going to describe a situation to you:*
> *you and your friend are planning to spend a weekend in London.*
> *Talk about what you have to organize before you leave.*
> *Decide which are the most important things that you want*
> *to do or see in London.*
> *Here are some pictures with some ideas to help you.*

Speaking Part 3: Describing a picture `Berlin` `Brandenburg`

> *Candidate A, here's your photo-*
> *graph. Please show it to candidate B and*
> *talk about what you can see there.*

> *Now candidate B, here's your photo-*
> *graph. Please show it to candidate A and*
> *talk about what you can see there.*

Speaking Part 4: Discussing a topic `Berlin` `Brandenburg`

> *You each saw a photograph of inner-city transportation.*
> *Some people think that cars should not be allowed to drive in city centres. What do you think:*
> *is this a good idea? Can you think of some reasons why people would suggest this?*
> *What would be the consequences for people's safety and for the environment?*
> *Would you ride your bicycle more if cars weren't allowed to drive in your city or town?*

MUSTERPRÜFUNG 2

Schriftliche Prüfung, Teil I: Hörverstehen `Berlin` `Brandenburg`

Listening Part 1: Short messages

_____ / 4

- *You are going to hear two short messages.*
- *You will hear the recording twice.*
- *There are four questions in this part, two questions for each message.*
- *Look at the pictures and then listen to the recording.*
- *Choose the correct picture and put a tick (✓) in the right box.*

Message one

1   Which bus did Mrs Jarvis catch?

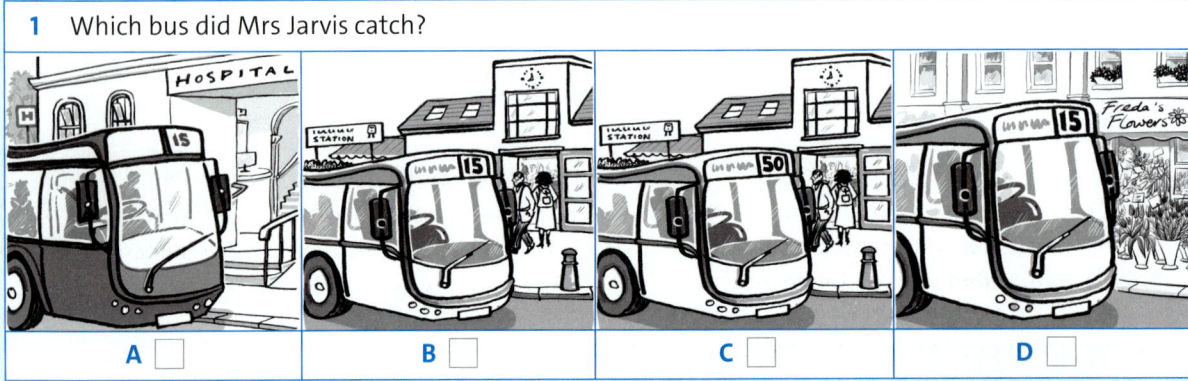

A ☐   B ☐   C ☐   D ☐

2   What had Mrs Jarvis lost?

A ☐   B ☐   C ☐   D ☐

Message two

3   What happened to Megan on the way to the party?

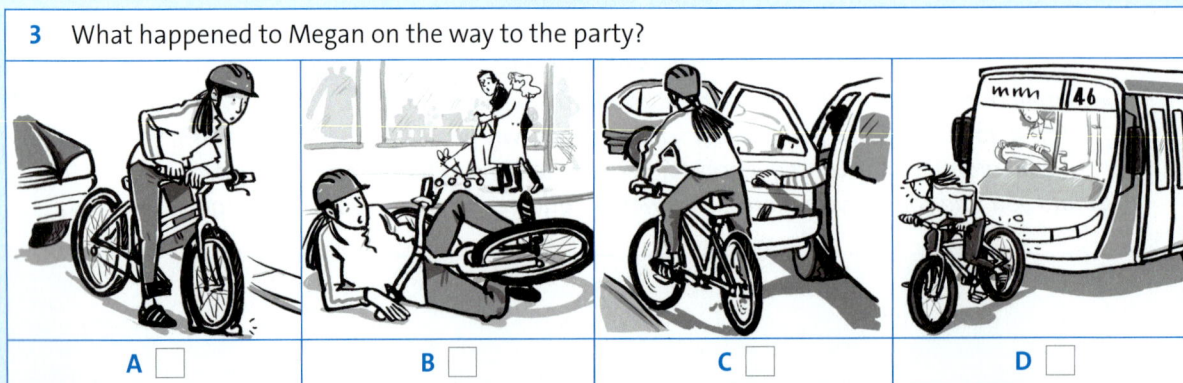

A ☐   B ☐   C ☐   D ☐

4 What happened next?

A ☐   B ☐   C ☐   D ☐

Listening Part 2: Radio ads

_____/4

- *Please note: You do not need to understand every word to do this task.*
- *You are going to hear four radio ads.*
- *You will hear the recording twice.*
- *Read the slogans below first, then listen to the recording.*
- *For each ad choose the correct slogan from the list (A–F) and put a tick (✓) in the right box.*
- *There is only one correct slogan for each ad.*
- *Two slogans can't be matched.*

A Work at sea.

B Please be aware of the new system!

C Hot drinks are good for you.

D Book your cruise holiday now!

E Be safe – take action now!

F Think of your weight.

		Slogan					
Number	Radio ads	A	B	C	D	E	F
5	Radio ad 1	☐	☐	☐	☐	☐	☐
6	Radio ad 2	☐	☐	☐	☐	☐	☐
7	Radio ad 3	☐	☐	☐	☐	☐	☐
8	Radio ad 4	☐	☐	☐	☐	☐	☐

Listening Part 3: Three British planes

_____ / 9

23

- *You are going to hear three people talking about their favourite British planes.*
- *You will hear the recording twice.*
- *Complete the table below. Use 1 to 5 words or numbers.*

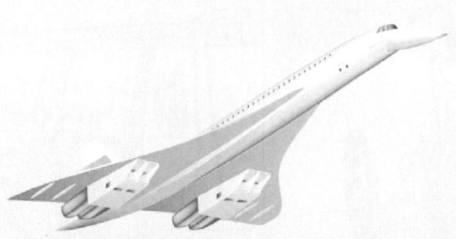

Name of plane	When did it fly?	Special because ...	Taken out of service because ...
Short Empire	9 in the *(years)*	10	11
Comet	12 first passenger flight *(date)*:	13	14
Concorde	15 from *(year)* to *(year)*	16	17

*Listening Part 4: Cricket in India

_____ / 8

24

- *You are going to hear a radio interview about the sport of cricket and the role of India in the sport.*
- *You will hear the recording twice.*
- *Read the statements below first, then listen to the recording.*
- *Put a tick (✓) in the box next to the correct statement.*
- *Only one statement is correct in each case.*

18 Aarav Malhotra's question is which two sports	A	☐	have the most players in the world.
	B	☐	are played in the most countries in the world.
	C	☐	have the most fans in the world.

19 If we don't count young children, then	A	☐	a large majority of all the people in the world are football fans.
	B	☐	almost 50% of all the people in the world are football fans.
	C	☐	a little more than 50% of all the people in the world are football fans.

20 The number of countries participating in the Cricket World Cup	A	☐	has fallen between 2007 and 2015.
	B	☐	has risen with every tournament.
	C	☐	is bigger than the number of countries participating in the Basketball World Cup.

21 India	A	☐	has won the Cricket World Cup more often than any other country.
	B	☐	is more successful than Australia in world cricket.
	C	☐	is almost as successful as Australia in world cricket.

22 England	A	☐	has won the Cricket World Cup twice.
	B	☐	is the country where cricket was born.
	C	☐	is more successful at international cricket than India.

23 The cricket players who earn the most money	A	☐	are Indian and play in India.
	B	☐	are Europeans and Americans who play in India.
	C	☐	were once Indian, but not anymore.

India's Rohit Sharma during the ICC Champions Trophy in Cardiff, Wales (2013)

24 The money in Indian cricket comes from	A	☐	sponsors in Europe.
	B	☐	fans in Europe and North America.
	C	☐	companies' advertisements in India.

25 According to Aarav, people in countries that don't play cricket	A	☐	think that cricket is exciting.
	B	☐	don't really know how cricket is played.
	C	☐	both A + B

Schriftliche Prüfung, Teil II: **Leseverstehen/Schreiben** `Berlin`

Reading Part 1: Summer jobs
_____ / 10

> - *These people (a–e) are all looking for a summer job.*
> - *First read the information about the people, then look at the descriptions of the jobs (A–H)*
>   *on page 61.*
> - *In each case find the **two** jobs the people would like to do. Write the letters of the jobs in the boxes*
>   *next to the people's names.*
> - *Some of the jobs can be chosen more than once.*

No.	Job 1	Job 2	The people
1/2			a) **Kylie** (19) likes the outdoors and is keen on climbing, hiking and water sports. She is outspoken and has never been afraid to take up causes, whether they were popular or not. She is a passionate vegan, for example, as an expression of her respect for the environment and for the welfare of animals. But while Kylie is always ready to argue her case, she is also a good listener, and for this reason gets on well with all kinds of people.
3/4			b) **Abdul** (18) spent most of his childhood in Afghanistan before he came to Britain a few years ago. He has always loved nature and wishes to study botany at university. Therefore he could imagine working in a park or garden, but he would also be happy to help elderly people or people with mental health issues. The main thing is that it should be full-time work – and he would not mind driving to work, as he has a driving license.
5/6			c) **Simona** (17) is originally from Spain, although she and her family have lived in Sheffield for five years now and she speaks English with a nice Yorkshire accent! She is a high-flyer who likes to mix with people in high places. Her dream career is marketing, but maybe surprisingly her favourite hobby is gardening. She has green fingers and loves outdoor work. She is flexible as to which days she can work, but can only commit to part-time work this summer.
7/8			d) **Andy** (18) is a good all-rounder – good at sport and interested in science. He loves taking out his camera and taking portraits of his friends and family. And he manages all this even though he is taking driving lessons with the aim of taking his test in October. Andy is patient and considerate, and looks after his elderly grandpa – good informal experience for a summer job in social work or care for somebody recovering from an accident.

| 9/10 | | |  | **e)** Jessica (17) is an open, friendly student. Her ideal afternoon? Being outside in the hills, by a river or waterfall, taking photos. It's her favourite hobby and when she leaves school she hopes to be able to focus on photography at college. Jessica is also something of a sports freak, and could imagine doing a summer job in which she can do something sporty with children. |

A Grasper Plc   We are currently recruiting for a door-to-door charity fundraiser which raises money for the British Pony Trust. This is a great opportunity to work on behalf of an organisation that cares for ponies across the UK. We will train you in your role and prepare you for what you can expect on the doorstep. You will be part of a team, with other members also working in your area. This is a job for a caring person with a good command of English. All fundraisers must be over 18 years of age.

B The **Sheffield Parks Division** needs helpers for the current restoration of three Victorian parks across the city. Your task will be to support our team of professional botanists and park keepers, and the majority of your work will be outside. It will involve planting trees and flowers, weeding, digging, and similar tasks. These part-time jobs, paid at a rate of £8.50 an hour, will be available from the beginning of May to the end of September.

C Here at **GreatCare UK** we provide a range of home services for elderly people who need help in order to continue living in their own homes. This might include washing or dressing elderly people, preparing a simple meal, or simply sitting down to chat with them. Our assistants cover a considerable area of Sheffield and frequently need to drive from one customer to the next. A driving license is therefore essential, and we pay you for your travel time. Applicants must be 18 or over. Please apply and supply a CV online.

D Premium Hospitality   Do you fancy working with film and music stars in some of the best venues in town? Then look no further. We specialize in hospitality at concerts and film premieres, so this is a unique opportunity to see what goes on backstage at Sheffield's most exclusive star-studded events. As a member of our team you will help us look after our VIPs and their guests. This is not a full-time position, and you will be required to work at short notice. In return we'll look after you while you work with us by offering you full training and good rates of pay.

E Clovis is a registered charity that offers work to all people including people with learning disabilities. We grow and sell a wide range of seasonal organic fruit, vegetables and plants in pots including bedding plants, cottage garden perennials and herbs. For the coming months we have full-time work available maintaining churchyards and restoring and tidying individuals' gardens. Please phone for details.

F PicPac   Become that person that captures and records amazing moments! We work in the leisure, theme park and tourist industries, and our aim is to allow visitors to keep their memories and share them with friends, family and the world. We offer our customers a wide choice of formats for memorable pictures, whether digitally, in print, on mugs and plates, on T-shirts, etc. We are always on the lookout for talented people who are able to capture the moment with a camera.

G Peak District Activity Centres   Our Activity Assistants help our Activity Instructors train groups of children in outdoor activities such as abseiling, canoeing, rock-climbing, etc. They help with the evening entertainment and are prepared to do other tasks including cleaning and serving meals. We are ideally looking for people who can commit to full-time work and have an NGB qualification. But if you don't have a qualification yet, don't worry! Our non-qualified assistants receive training and are not required to take full responsibility for activities.

H The lives of many sick and aged people can be dramatically transformed by providing them with just an hour or two of help a day. That is our aim here at **LocalSocial**. With funds from local sponsors we pay for our workers to visit elderly people near their homes, and to help with whatever needs doing. It could be helping people to go to the local shop, or simply providing company over a cup of tea. If you believe that everybody deserves a chance to live an independent life, this is the job for you.

Reading Part 2: Short texts _____ / 6

> - *Look at the text and the statements in each task.*
> - *Put a tick (✓) next to the statement that matches the text – A, B, C or D.*
> - *There is only one correct statement for each sign.*

Baxter and sons – your local professional plumber

With a response time of within 30-90 minutes* in the local area, we are second to none for emergency plumbing services.

Our trained operators provide free quotes and estimates for any plumbing work. No job too small.

We don't charge a call-out fee, so you only pay the price that we quote.

* where possible

11

A	☐	This company is looking for a professional plumber.
B	☐	This company is looking for trainees for small jobs.
C	☐	This company offers fast plumbing services.
D	☐	This company offers the cheapest rates in town.

Lost puppy

Pooch is a small Terrier puppy, last seen near the playground in Ambrose Street on 27th November.
Pooch is very friendly and likes to be patted – but he doesn't always answer to his name.
Please help us find him!
Small financial reward given.

Phone 07998 934 501
Thank you

12

A	☐	Somebody wants to sell a pet to a friendly new owner.
B	☐	Somebody is looking to buy a friendly little dog.
C	☐	Somebody is looking for a runaway dog.
D	☐	Somebody found a pet and is trying to find the owner.

Bike Bag Phone Holder – with rain cover

THREE straps will keep the bag firmly in place.

The APVC screen allows you to operate your phone as normal while it is in the case.

Suitable for phones measuring up to 15 cm x 7 cm

The phone holder includes separate storage space beneath for cycling essentials.

The phone case portion of the holder is tightly connected to the top with Velcro, and can be easily removed when you leave your bike, leaving the storage bag still strapped to your bike.

www.beyondbikes.com

13 What is special about this product?

A	☐	You can use your phone without taking it out of this phone holder.
B	☐	This phone case is firmly attached to your bike and can't be stolen.
C	☐	This phone holder is adapted to fit all mobile phones.
D	☐	This phone case is smaller than any other phone cases on the market.

Front of House Staff

Ricardo Eatery, Falmouth
£6.50 – £8 an hour

We are currently hiring team members to serve customers in our busy restaurant.
Experience preferred, but not essential.
Applicants must have a positive attitude and be friendly with customers.

We offer:
· Excellent tips.
· Training and professional development within your chosen field of hospitality.
· Accommodation on the premises.

Please send an email with a copy of your CV and a contact telephone number to:
team@ricardoeatery.co.uk

Job type: Full-time

14

A	☐	The restaurant will only hire people who have worked in a restaurant before.
B	☐	If you take the job you will be able to live at the restaurant.
C	☐	The job is mostly kitchen work.
D	☐	The restaurant is looking for volunteers to help out.

Passengers must familiarize themselves with the procedures in the event of an emergency on board the ship.

The emergency signal consists of seven short blasts from the ship's whistle followed by one long blast. If the emergency signal is sounded, all passengers should proceed to the nearest muster station. Keep calm and do not run. Avoid panic.

The muster stations are marked by a green circle with family members within it. In the event of an emergency, members of the crew will be at the muster stations to give passengers further information and to issue life-saving equipment if necessary.

15 In case of danger ...

A	☐	passengers should stay with their families at all times.
B	☐	passengers must return to their cabins.
C	☐	the crew will give a signal by flashing lights.
D	☐	passengers should meet in certain areas of the ship.

Tuesday 11th July at 8.00 pm
Jane Bradley
£16

Join Jane for an evening of high-energy fun! After a fully sold out show last year, Jane returns as part of her annual nationwide tour, with material that is topical and up to the minute. No one escapes her biting wit. This is a laugh-out-loud show that will have you rolling in the aisles and coming back for more.

16

A	☐	This notice is about a comedy show.
B	☐	This is a job offer for an artist's assistant.
C	☐	This is about a local charity event.
D	☐	The notice advertises a sports event.

*Reading Part 3: Life in South Africa today

_____ / 9

> • Read the text and the statements on page 65 – 66.
> • Put a tick (✓) in the box next to the correct answer.
> • Only one answer is correct in each case.

Society is constantly changing. That is true for all countries, but few have changed as radically as South Africa in the last twenty-five years. The critical event that brought on the change was the country's first free election in 1994. Before that, everything in your life depended on the colour of your skin. Under a system called *apartheid*, black and white people lived in different zones, went to different schools, had different jobs, relaxed on different beaches and even used different public toilets. Black people could not vote, and marriages between black and white people were forbidden. This system led to street protests by the black population, which were violently put down by the forces of the white government. Many unarmed protesters were killed, many more were locked up in prison.

The election of Nelson Mandela, South Africa's first black president, in 1994 put an end to all that. *Apartheid* was abolished and all South

Africans – black, white and Asian – now enjoy equal rights. Nine African languages, including Zulu (the first language of over 20% of South Africans!), have joined English and Afrikaans (a language brought to South Africa by Dutch settlers) as official languages. This means that most local communities can send their children to schools which teach in their own language. English is a minority language in terms of first language, but it's the language of trade and the media, and the language that allows people of different ethnic groups to communicate. It is this wide range of cultures, languages and ethnic backgrounds, rather than the climate or the sometimes colourful way of dressing, that has earned South Africa the nickname of the *Rainbow Nation*.

But changes for the better are coming too slowly for many black South Africans. The white population (nine percent of the total population) still owns a larger proportion of the country's wealth than black South Africans, who make up 80 percent of the population. True, there is now a small number of black people who have become rich, but 54 percent of the black population live in poverty, according to a government report from 2014, compared to 0.8 percent of the white population.

You can see this inequality in education, too. Schools in mostly white areas of the country are well equipped, while many schools in mostly black areas have poor facilities – like too few computers or even too few toilets. And schools teaching in one of the official African languages often find it difficult to employ teachers who can speak their language.

Life is particularly hard for the girls because they suffer most from the violence in the streets. About one third of girls experience sexual violence before the age of 18. The rates of HIV infections are high, and over 60 percent of the victims are women. Many children have to manage life on their own because their parents die young, and they often have to leave school in order to look after younger brothers and sisters.

South Africa's economy is now growing by less than two percent a year, which is a lower increase than in the first years of the 21st century. This means that the government now has less money than before to spend on improving schools and social conditions. But South Africa's problems should not be exaggerated. The economy is the biggest in Africa after Nigeria, and incomes per person are among the highest in Africa. South Africa's middle class grew by an extraordinary 250% between 2004 and 2012.

However, while conditions have generally improved for most people, and blacks can now go onto beaches and into bars that were once reserved for whites, life is still hard for many black South Africans. The gap between the standard of living of black and white South Africans is as large as ever, so it's not surprising that more and more blacks are becoming impatient for more change.

17 The writer's opinion is that life in South Africa	A	☐	has changed less than in most countries.
	B	☐	has changed about the same as in most countries.
	C	☐	has changed more than in most countries.
	D	☐	has not changed much in the last few years.

18 Under *apartheid* black people	A	☐	could take part in elections, but couldn't marry white people.
	B	☐	could take part in elections, but couldn't go to the same beaches as white people.
	C	☐	couldn't take part in elections, but could marry white people.
	D	☐	couldn't take part in elections and couldn't marry white people.

19 As far as languages are concerned, it is true that	A	☐	a small majority of South Africans speak English as a first language.
	B	☐	a majority of South Africans speak Zulu.
	C	☐	South Africa has eleven official languages.
	D	☐	Afrikaans is a language that was first spoken by black South Africans.

20 South Africa is sometimes called the *Rainbow Nation* because	A	☐	the country celebrates its multicultural society.
	B	☐	people wear very colourful clothes.
	C	☐	it has a climate with a high number of rainbows.
	D	☐	rainbows are important in traditional stories.

21 The situation today, according to the text, is that	A	☐	black South Africans now have more money than white South Africans.
	B	☐	about half of black South Africans are poor.
	C	☐	only 0.8 percent of the white population are still rich.
	D	☐	most South Africans feel that conditions are changing fast enough.

22 Schools in mostly black areas are at a disadvantage because	A	☐	the equipment is not as good as in "white" schools.
	B	☐	it's hard to find English-speaking staff.
	C	☐	the students protest against inequality.
	D	☐	both **A + B**

23 Many South African children can't go to school because	A	☐	this is what their culture expects of them.
	B	☐	they have too much to do at home.
	C	☐	many schools don't have enough toilets.
	D	☐	there's too much violence.

24	A	☐	had more money to spend than it did later.
In the first years of the 21st century, the South African government	B	☐	could not spend as much money as it did later.
	C	☐	could spend less on schools than today.
	D	☐	was still trying to enforce *apartheid*.

25	A	☐	have the biggest economy in Africa.
Today, South Africans	B	☐	earn less than in most African countries.
	C	☐	enjoy a better life than they did in 1994.
	D	☐	all have more or less the same standard of living.

Schriftliche Prüfung, Teil II: Leseverstehen/Schreiben Berlin

Writing Part 1: Your photo
_____ / 5

- *You have posted this photo.*
- *Your friend Jana wants to know more.*
- *Answer her questions.*
- *Write 30–50 words.*

What do you say to that?

Wow, who is this lucky person?
Doesn't look like you ...

Are you celebrating or something?

Tell me more!

Writing Part 2: How fit are you?

Inhalt: _____ / 6   Sprache: _____ / 6

- *Read what a blogger has written below.*
- *Then write back, answering all of his questions.*
- *Write a minimum of 100 words.*

● ● ●

www.young-and-lively.com

Name:
FitForFun

We all know that we should do more sport or fitness exercises. We know that regular physical activity is essential for good health. So the question is: why do so few of us do it?
I'd be interested to hear your experiences of doing sports, whether positive or negative. Do you follow the health experts' advice and work out on a regular basis? Or do you dislike physical activity? Are you too busy to do sports? Or too lazy? Or do you – like me ☺ – enjoy sports for fun instead of seeing it as a duty?

Writing Part 3: Mediation – A warm welcome

_____ / 8

Adnan is a new boy in your class. He is from Syria and is trying to find out where he and his family could get advice or meet German people, for example while doing sport together. His English is still better than his German.

- *Read the two adverts.*
- *Choose **one** advert.*
- *Write an email to Adnan and tell him what is on offer.*
- *Mention at least four points that might be of interest to Adnan and his family.*
- ***Do not translate word for word**, just give the main information.*
- *Write complete sentences.*

Lichtblick Kontakt- und Beratungsstellen

Wir betreiben in unserer Stadt drei Lichtblick Kontakt- und Beratungsstellen. Unsere ehrenamtlichen Mitarbeiter ermöglichen mit ihrem unermüdlichen Einsatz ein breites Hilfsangebot. Die Standorte Mitte und Nord öffnen ihre Türen an 365 Tagen im Jahr, der Standort Süd an jedem Werktag.

Unsere Kontakt- und Beratungsstellen bieten ein offenes Angebot, und gerade diese Offenheit erleichtert es vielen Menschen, den Weg zu uns zu finden. Bei uns findet jeder, egal ob alt oder jung, Verständnis und erhält Rat und Information.

Besonders beliebt ist der Lichtblick Mittagstisch, der in unseren Standorten Mitte und Süd stattfindet. Hier wird der erste Kontakt zu unseren Mitarbeitern und zu anderen Besuchern schnell und informell geknüpft, zu weiteren Gesprächen und Hilfen ist es dann nur ein kleiner Schritt.

In der Kontakt- und Beratungsstelle Mitte gibt es darüber hinaus spezielle Angebote für Menschen mit Migrationshintergrund. Die Beratung kann in türkischer, arabischer und serbischer Sprache erfolgen.

Der Standort Nord bietet jeden Sonntag betreute Lichtblick Spielgruppen für kleine (2–6 Jahre) oder größere (7–10 Jahre) Kinder an.

Menschen mit psychischer Erkrankung oder Sucht finden in allen drei Kontakt- und Beratungsstellen einfühlsame und kompetente Ansprechpartner.

Für die Menschen, die unsere Hilfe benötigen, aber nicht selbst zu uns kommen können, bieten wir kurzfristige und kostenlose Hausbesuche zur Beratung oder Betreuung an. Ein Anruf genügt, um den Kreis der Isolation zu durchbrechen.

www.lichtblick-für-dich.de

Sport im Park

Du brauchst kein Fitnessstudio, um dich in der Stadt fit zu halten! Komm einfach jeden Samstagvormittag in den Konrad-Adenauer-Park und trainiere kostenlos mit einem unserer ausgebildeten Trainer.

Der Kreisjugendring organisiert dort zwischen 8 Uhr und 12 Uhr ein umfassendes Programm für interessierte Menschen jeden Alters. Von Zirkeltraining über Tai-Chi und Zumba bis hin zu Pilates und Yoga ist alles im Angebot. Bring einfach bequeme Kleidung, ein Handtuch oder eine Matte und etwas zu trinken mit. Wir sorgen dann für Bälle, Netze usw., für motivierende Musik und die richtigen Bewegungsabläufe.

Sport im Park ist gratis, aber es ist ratsam, sich online zu registrieren und einen festen Platz zu buchen (pro Gruppe nicht mehr als 20 Teilnehmer). Mit etwas Glück kann man aber auch spontan einen Platz finden, falls ein Angemeldeter nicht erschienen ist. Es lohnt sich also, einfach vorbeizuschauen!

Sport im Park wird auch in den Ferien angeboten, nicht jedoch bei Regen.

www.sport-im-park.de

Mündliche Prüfung

Speaking Part 1: Warming up `Berlin` `Brandenburg`

Answer these questions about yourself.

> Hello. Can you tell me your name, please, and how you spell it?

> How do you get to school every day?

> And what's the weather like today?

> How are you today?

> How long does it take you?

> When will you arrive home this afternoon?

Speaking Part 2: Agreeing and disagreeing `Berlin`

> I'm going to describe a situation to you: you and your friend are planning a party. You have hired a big hall with a kitchen, and all the students in your year are invited.
>
> Talk about what you will have to organize for the party.
>
> Decide which are the most important things to buy.
>
> Here are some pictures with some ideas to help you.

Speaking Part 3: Describing a picture `Berlin` `Brandenburg`

A

> Candidate A, here's your photograph. Please show it to candidate B and talk about what you can see.

B

> Now candidate B, here's your photograph. Please show it to candidate A and talk about what you can see.

Speaking Part 4: Discussing a topic `Berlin` `Brandenburg`

> Your photographs showed photos of people at work. What is more important in a job: doing a job that you like or earning a lot of money?

Tipps für die Prüfung

Prüfungsvorbereitung

- **Beginne rechtzeitig mit dem Lernen und mache dir einen Lernplan**, bei dem du auch Wiederholungsphasen einplanst. Starte mit Aufgaben, die dir im Unterricht noch schwerfallen. Hake ab, was du bereits erledigt hast.

- **Überlege dir, wo du im Englischen noch grundsätzliche Probleme oder Lücken hast** (z. B. Grammatikprobleme, die immer wieder auftreten). Diese Themen kannst du dann mit den interaktiven Übungen auf www.scook.de gezielt noch einmal wiederholen.

- **Mache dich mit dem Ablauf der Prüfung und mit allen Aufgabenformaten vertraut.** Plane im Vorfeld, wie viel Zeit du für jeden Prüfungsteil und für die Kontrolle zur Verfügung hast.

- **Schreibe dir auf, wann und wo die Prüfung stattfindet**, und plane etwas mehr Zeit für den Weg ein als sonst.

- **Lege alle Materialien am Vorabend der Prüfung bereit** (z. B. funktionstüchtige Stifte, Uhr; Smartphones sind nicht erlaubt!).

- **Achte auf ausreichend Schlaf und ein gutes Frühstück.**

Wenn du dich gut vorbereitet hast, kannst du selbstbewusst in die Prüfung gehen!

Während der Prüfung

- **Behalte die Zeit im Blick!** Am besten legst du während der Prüfung eine Uhr auf den Tisch und schaust von Zeit zu Zeit darauf. Wenn du an einer Aufgabe festhängst, gehe lieber erstmal zur nächsten Frage weiter. Nimm dir am Ende einige Minuten Zeit, um deine Antworten noch einmal durchzugehen.

- **Lies die Aufgabenstellung gründlich durch**, bevor du mit der Bearbeitung beginnst. Manchmal enthält eine Aufgabe mehrere Teilaspekte. Markiere sie und übersetze sie dir zur Sicherheit in deine Muttersprache.

- **Nutze deine Chance!** Auch wenn du unsicher bist, ob die Lösung stimmt, so ist es ratsam, die Aufgabe trotzdem zu bearbeiten. So hast du zumindest eine Chance, dass es richtig ist. Kreuzt du keine Lösung an oder lässt die Lücke leer, so bekommst du auf jeden Fall null Punkte.

- **Mache dir bei Schreibaufgaben Notizen, wenn du gut in der Zeit liegst.** Sie können dir helfen, deine Gedanken zu ordnen und deinen Text sinnvoll zu strukturieren. Beachte aber, dass nur dein endgültiger Text in die Bewertung eingeht.

- **Gib deinen Texten eine gute Struktur mit Einleitung, Hauptteil und Schluss.** Beginne jeden neuen Textteil mit einem neuen Absatz.

- **Formuliere klare Sätze.** Vermeide es, komplizierte deutsche Sätze wortwörtlich ins Englische zu übersetzen. Formuliere möglichst mit deinen eigenen Worten.

- **Kontrolliere am Ende**, was du geschrieben hast. Achte besonders auf Vollständigkeit, die Rechtschreibung, die Zeitformen deiner Verben und den Satzbau.

Wir wünschen dir viel Erfolg für deine Prüfung!

Übersicht über die Aufgaben zum Hörverstehen

Die Tonaufnahmen (MP3-Dateien) und die Hörtexte findest du online unter www.scook.de.
Deinen persönlichen Zugangscode findest du auf Seite 1 deines Abschlussprüfungstrainers.

Track	Kapitel	Titel	Seite
1	Training Section	Listening Part 1: Short messages	7
2	Training Section	Listening Part 2: Radio ads	8
3	Training Section	Listening Part 3: Calgary's skyways	9
4	Training Section	Listening Part 4: A visit to Krakow	9
5	Training Section	Listening: The Niagara Falls (Version 1)	10
6	Training Section	Listening: The Niagara Falls (Version 2)	12
7	Training Section	Listening: The Tour de Yorkshire	13
8	Training Section	Listening: Three tourist attractions in Brighton	14
9	Training Section	Speaking Part 1: Warming up (Prüfungsbeispiel 1)	36
10	Training Section	Speaking Part 1: Warming up (Prüfungsbeispiel 2)	36
11	Training Section	Speaking Part 2: Agreeing and disagreeing (Prüfungsbeispiel 1)	36
12	Training Section	Speaking Part 2: Agreeing and disagreeing (Prüfungsbeispiel 2)	37
13	Training Section	Speaking Part 3: Describing a picture (Prüfungsbeispiel 1)	37
14	Training Section	Speaking Part 3: Describing a picture (Prüfungsbeispiel 2)	38
15	Training Section	Speaking Part 4: Discussing a topic (Prüfungsbeispiel 1)	38
16	Training Section	Speaking Part 4: Discussing a topic (Prüfungsbeispiel 2)	39
17	Musterprüfung 1	Listening Part 1: Short messages	41
18	Musterprüfung 1	Listening Part 2: Radio ads	42
19	Musterprüfung 1	Listening Part 3: William Shakespeare	43
20	Musterprüfung 1	Listening Part 4: Bo-Kaap – a special district in Cape Town	43
21	Musterprüfung 2	Listening Part 1: Short messages	56
22	Musterprüfung 2	Listening Part 2: Radio ads	57
23	Musterprüfung 2	Listening Part 3: Three British planes	58
24	Musterprüfung 2	Listening Part 4: Cricket in India	58
25	Urheberrechtserklärung		

Studio: Clarity Studio Berlin
Regie und Aufnahmeleitung: Christian Schmitz
Tontechnik: Christian Marx, Pascal Thinius